How to Analyze
and Overcome Your Fears

Other Books by Stella Terrill Mann

CHANGE YOUR LIFE THROUGH PRAYER

CHANGE YOUR LIFE THROUGH LOVE

CHANGE YOUR LIFE THROUGH FAITH AND WORK

HOW TO USE THE POWER OF YOUR WORD

HOW TO LIVE IN THE CIRCLE OF PRAYER

How to Analyze and Overcome Your Fears

STELLA TERRILL MANN

DeVorss & Co., *Publishers*
P.O. Box 550
Marina del Rey, California 90291

3RD PAPERBACK EDITION 1978

COPYRIGHT © 1962 BY STELLA TERRILL MANN
ALL RIGHTS RESERVED
NO PART OF THIS BOOK MAY BE REPRODUCED IN ANY FORM
WITHOUT PERMISSION IN WRITING FROM THE PUBLISHER

LIBRARY OF CONGRESS CATALOG CARD NUMBER: 61-15984

ISBN: 0-87516-175-8

PRINTED IN THE UNITED STATES OF AMERICA
BY BOOK GRAPHICS, INC.

*To my dear Aunt Harriet Schellenger Jay,
whose love, faith and good works have kept
her happy, young and free from fear for
eighty-seven years*

Contents

1. IF YOU CAN ANALYZE YOUR FEARS YOU CAN OVERCOME THEM   1
   Story from Life: *The Woman Who Lived with a Ghost*

2. OVERCOMING FEARS CONCERNING MONEY, SECURITY AND PROSPERITY   18
   Story from Life: *The Man Who Thought He Was a Grasshopper*

3. OVERCOMING FEARS CONCERNING LOVE, MARRIAGE AND OTHER HUMAN RELATIONS PROBLEMS   36
   Story from Life: *The Woman Who Gorged Herself on Apples of Fear*

4. OVERCOMING FEARS CONCERNING LIBERTY AND FREEDOM   51
   Story from Life: *The Man Who Lived in a Cage*

5. OVERCOMING FEARS CONCERNING THE SECOND HALF OF LIFE   70
   Story from Life: *The Woman Who Looked Back*

6. OVERCOMING FEARS OF DEATH AND THE BEYOND   86
   Story from Life: *The Man Who Was Afraid of His Shadow*

7. OVERCOMING FEARS OF TOMORROW IN OUR
TROUBLED WORLD OF TODAY 106
Report from Life: *They Have a Dream in Their Heart*

8. THERE ARE NO FEARS BEYOND YOUR CONTROL 132
Story from Life: *The Man Who Lived with Monsters*

9. LAND BEYOND THE DARKNESS 145

10. HOW TO GET THE MOST OUT OF THIS BOOK 162

How to Analyze
and Overcome Your Fears

1

If You Can Analyze Your Fears You Can Overcome Them

Fear is the world's number one problem . . . most of our fears are hidden . . . take a constructive and fearless look at fear . . . you can't have fear and good health too.

STORY FROM LIFE:
The Woman Who Lived with a Ghost

> *"Fear is the painful emotion caused by a sense of impending danger, or evil; dread."*
> WEBSTER

Working with people with problems for more than twenty-five years has convinced me that *fear gives rise to more trouble in the life and affairs of the individual than all other causes put together.* And yet:

The hardest part of my job as a religious counselor in helping others to help themselves is to get them to face their hidden fears. For fear often is the real trouble, the underlying cause and not the problem they have come to talk about, which actually is the outgrowth or effect that the hidden, unrecognized fear has produced.

Therefore, the first step in overcoming fear is to *analyze* the problem we face to uncover possible hidden fears. When found, we handle them in the same way that we handle the open or recognized fears. But most of our fears are hidden. For example:

Let me tell you about *the woman who lived with a ghost*.

This lady, whom we can call Mrs. Pollard, obviously ill and suffering, came to me saying her doctor had told her frankly he could find nothing organically wrong with her, and suggested that she see a psychiatrist. But Mrs. Pollard had heard me lecture and had read several of my books. She came to ask if I would pray with her about her health and what she was sure was a threat of loss of her eyesight.

I explained to her that it is almost useless to pray concerning a problem until we have analyzed it and know for sure what it is we need to pray for and about. Since fear is the root of so much physical and mental illness, I asked her, "What is it that makes you afraid?"

At first she repeated there was nothing except fear of losing her health and eyesight. But when we got into her life story I discovered the fact that about a year earlier she had been afraid she was losing her husband's love to another woman. She tried many ways to hold his love but all of them failed. She then decided that if she could not have love she would settle for sympathy and pity in order to hold him by her side. She began to fake illness and failing eyesight. "Will you please drive me today, dear," she would say. "I'm afraid I'm losing my sight. I will be driving along, and suddenly, I just can't see."

Her husband was greatly concerned and became unusually attentive. Mrs. Pollard liked all that new concern and so she added an imaginary heart trouble to her illness list. Before very long she was convinced her husband had given up the other woman but she felt it necessary to continue her pretenses. In the meantime, the power of her word had started to deliver to her the conditions which she had described, pretended and talked about so vividly. She was not aware of the fact that she actually was asking for those conditions. She was daily and sometimes hourly using the creative power of her word in the form of saying, "It is so." This method of using our creative power can be far more effective when accompanied by deep feeling than the formal procedure of asking or commanding "Let there be!" Her fears had aroused deep feelings which were gaining control of her health.

This had gone on until now she had all the symptoms, and pains of the sicknesses she had pretended. The first tests showed her eyesight was good; that she had not outgrown her glasses. But now, for stretches at a time she could not see to read the newspaper, and she no longer drove her car.

Again, the first tests showed that she had no organic heart trouble. But now there were times when her heart skipped beats, pounded and "fluttered so that she felt faint." At other times severe pains "tore through her heart and raced down her arm until she was certain she was having a heart attack." She said she no longer feared losing her husband; that they had come to a new and good understanding which she felt would last. But she was afraid of losing her health and while she could not admit it at first, she was afraid of dying. For all ill health is a degree of walking through the Valley of the Shadow of Death. Ill health is a taste of death.

Now, the underlying cause of her trouble was this: Mrs. Pollard felt guilty for having deceived her husband, who was still very much concerned about her health. When her first doctor told him, "I have found nothing wrong with your wife," Mr. Pollard was angry, called the doctor incompetent and demanded that they find one who knew his business.

But Mrs. Pollard, feeling certain a second doctor would find the illnesses real, told her husband she did not want to trust another doctor; that she would rather try spiritual therapy. He was willing for her to come to me.

"I need an awful lot of prayer," the suffering woman sighed. "I know I have done wrong. I was living a lie in my deceit," she confessed.

But she could not bring herself to admit that she was afraid of displeasing God. She was unconsciously trying to punish herself in order to expiate her sense of guilt. Feelings are deeper than reason and do not stop to consult reason unless forced to do so. Mrs. Pollard actually felt that she was being made ill by God, as punishment. *Subconsciously she felt she deserved punishment.*

But in her conscious, reasoning mind, she wanted to be forgiven and restored to health, hence her requests for prayer.

"The answer to prayer depends upon faith," I explained and with this she could agree, having had Christian training. But she was not yet ready, able or willing to see that she first had to resolve her conflict before she could have much faith that her prayers could and would be answered.

My objective was to get her to see that she had to come to a firm decision: "I want to be sick and be punished and get rid of my sense of guilt"; or, "I want to get well and stay well." To do that she would have to recognize her basic fear, analyze it and then overcome it.

She wanted to continue talking about being afraid she might become an invalid and be confined to her room or to a hospital bed, or face the world without sight. To have permitted her to keep on talking in that way would have been to allow her to go around in a circle wearing her fear patterns into a deep rut.

I find that many people who have gone to psychiatrists, psychologists and other helpers have come to grief for that very reason: going around in a circle, failing to take a step out and up, and so wearing their rut into a deep ditch from which they then cannot climb out alone. This often is the result of failing to analyze the problem until the fear is found. Until it is found there is no basis for work. A great many earnest Christians whose health has not been restored through prayer become frustrated and give up prayer therapy. They either become resigned to ill health and say it is the will of God, or conclude there is no healing power in prayer. Mrs. Pollard was one of such people.

I finally got Mrs. Pollard to see she needed to face facts about her hidden and open fears. To do that, she would have to see clearly the false beliefs about life, the nature of God and man and their relationship, which had given rise to those fears. Since this is part of the method used in analyzing and overcoming all fear, it will help us to look into it thoroughly at this point.

My objective with Mrs. Pollard was to help her do the following:

1. *Analyze her problem* until the fear was uncovered.

Not all problems arise from fear. Sometimes a problem is the result of laziness, indifference, lack of accurate information or any one of many other causes. Problems of life are normal. They present opportunities for growth. Some problems present a happy challenge and contain no fear whatever. But Mrs. Pollard was definitely suffering from fear. So we needed to take all the steps.

2. *Analyze her fears* until we uncovered the false belief that gave rise to them. Because we never can get around this fact: all fear arises from a false belief.

3. *Find new information,* facts which she could accept and which together would give her a new belief and attitude toward herself, her problem and all life. This is

a process of learning the truth which will set the sufferer free from fear.

We studied together the *four basic false beliefs* which give rise to fear. They are:

1. Belief that there are *two powers* in the Universe, and that one of them is evil; for example, the belief that there is a God and a Devil. This belief gives rise to the fear that evil can and may overcome good.

2. Belief that there are *two sides to God's nature:* love and hate, and that the hate side can and may demand vengeance and give out punishment of an angry or jealous God. This gives rise to the fear of having displeased God, or that we will be punished or that we never can know the Will of God and so are doomed to suffer.

3. Belief that there is *no God*. This gives rise to the fear of final defeat of every desire of the heart; that all through life each man is at the mercy of all other men. Here the evil power resides in other men and in the natural world around us, and death ends all. This is the recognized Communist belief.

4. Belief that God or "some great power" does exist, but *man never can contact Him* or know Him. This is the belief known as separation. It gives rise to the fear of being inadequate to the problems of life, of competition with others and of loneliness. It often is the cause of deep melancholy, mental illness and crime and in instances leads to suicide. Here the evil power resides in others, circumstances, nature, with no help to be had

from God.

But regardless of which of the four basic false beliefs is held consciously or unconsciously, the net belief is the same: *that evil can overcome good*. This belief gives rise to fear, the "painful emotion caused by a sense of impending danger or evil."

After much discussion of the four basic false beliefs, I asked Mrs. Pollard whether she believed in a personal devil.

"No," she protested impatiently. "I don't believe in the devil or hell or anything like that. I got over that superstition years ago. It belongs to the dark ages."

"But you believe you deserve punishment?"

"Yes. All wrongdoing should be punished. We punish our children when they are disobedient or bad. We must, if we are to train them."

"Who or what is to do the punishing in your case?" I asked.

"God," she answered unhesitatingly.

"Then you believe there are two sides to God's nature, one of love and one of hate or vengeance?"

We discussed that point at great length. We consulted the New Testament, statements of modern science and our own common sense. We even tested our belief about God and man's relationship to Him in comparison with our belief about the ideal relationship between earth parents and children.

As Mrs. Pollard accepted idea after idea the expression on her face and in her eyes began to change from confusion and suffering to that of intense curiosity and hope. After a while she said:

"Yes, but if God does not punish us for wrongdoing how can the world be kept a safe, fit place to live in? We couldn't do without police and laws and jails," she argued.

"The spiritual laws under which we live on earth were all set up before man's time here began," I said. "These laws are self-executing. Wherever we find power we find laws under which it operates. You used the creative power of your word to bring sickness upon yourself under the law of cause and effect. You spoke the word for sickness. You acted it out. You pictured it. You declared it to be so. It had to become manifest."

"You mean I am punishing myself instead of God punishing me?"

"Yes, on two counts," I replied. "First, through wrong use of the creative power and second because you really want to be punished. We all need status with God because we all want eternal life. How can we achieve our heart's desire if God does not love us? There is a deeper cause back of your desire to be punished. You have developed spiritually to the place of wanting to cooperate with God's Project, Man. Your desire for punishment is a form of saying you are sorry for your wrongdoing and want God to accept your love and include you in His plans. You want to pay for your misdeeds so that you can feel free again."

To that, Mrs. Pollard finally could agree. But she

also asked, "How can I stop punishing myself?" Once again she wanted to talk about her fears of loss of health and eyesight and of being confined to a sick bed. After again warning her she must stop picturing the conditions she did not want, and to stop accepting into her mind any condition she did not want in her body, and to start to picture those conditions she did deserve, we went back to our work.

"The Bible tells us that to resolve such problems as yours we must confess, repent and seek salvation," I said. I explained to Mrs. Pollard that the original meaning of those words was not what theology has built up around them, but simply to talk over the problem with God and another person, to make a sober turning of the mind and then to go back in thought and feeling to that place of peace and happiness which the belief in a God of love gives us.

Mrs. Pollard needed to feel that God already had forgiven her before she had asked, even before she had disobeyed God by breaking the law of love. She had to see that the only change necessary was within her own mind, to come to an understanding with God, to know that all was right between her and God her Father Creator. Such understanding would dissolve her fears, because it is psychologically impossible to be at one with the good we desire and at the same time to know fear. The great rule in overcoming fear is to remember:

If we had no desires we would have no fears.

Therefore:

To feel absolutely certain that we will receive the good we desire is to dissolve fear.

In this first chapter we are laying the groundwork for analyzing and overcoming all our fears. It is advisable to take another look at the principle involved before going on with Mrs. Pollard's story.

In the final analysis fear is a feeling we will not get the good we desire, or that something bad is going to happen that we do not want to happen but are powerless to prevent. As soon as we know how to obtain the good, or to prevent the bad from happening, the fear is transformed into hope which then sets up some form of action —physical, mental or spiritual and generally all three. The more action that takes place the higher faith rises, for the flow of energy has been reversed with the reversal of belief. This continues until the problem is solved. We then move along on a plateau until some other situation arises which threatens our good. This starts another circle of fear to faith to accomplishment and peace. Or so it has been for generations but here we are going to learn how to handle it briefly, fully and so repeatedly that overcoming fear becomes an automatic habit for us.

It took considerable time and effort but Mrs. Pollard finally was ready for the prayers for which she had come. We read again:

"If we confess our sins he is faithful and just to forgive us our sins, and to cleanse us from all unrighteousness." (I John 1:9)

Our prayer was a simple, childlike confession and

asking of forgiveness. We also expressed our love, joy and gratitude for the love of God which is beyond our human understanding and for our gratitude for Mrs. Pollard's having become aware of truth that had set her free from fear and would continue to do so.

After our prayers Mrs. Pollard "felt much better." But she still was troubled in spirit. She had accepted the fact that she must sin no more lest a worse thing come upon her; that once we have been healed through a knowledge and use of spiritual laws we no longer can plead ignorance of the law. To attempt to do so is to set up more sense of guilt and fears. All this she understood so I asked her what was still troubling her.

"Will the ghost I have been living with all these months continue to haunt me?" she asked. "I am afraid my husband might find out the truth and that he would think ill of me the rest of my life. That would hurt more than giving him up to another woman."

"The thing to do with a troublesome ghost," I said, "is to dissolve it. Fears do create ghosts of things and conditions in our minds which we do not want in our lives. These can all be dissolved by vibrations of high faith and love. Not to do so is to run the danger of putting life into them. The Bible warns us that the power to do this rests in our own mouth, in our own word. This is the power by which the word becomes flesh. It is a good power, given to every man who has reached the status of free will. It is part of man's dominion given to him by God. We cannot turn the power off. So we must learn to use it to create good or suffer the consequences of creating unwanted things and conditions."

In her fears, Mrs. Pollard had mentally been seeing the look of revulsion on her husband's face, should he learn of her deceit. She had been hearing his words of condemnation. She had been thinking and picturing how she would fare in the world without him. All this was the body of her ghost. She had to start picturing her husband's great joy at her complete healing, to hear his words of gratitude for the power of prayer. She was to plan happy times with her husband, to think, see, feel, hear and know that all was well between them, just as all was now well between herself and God. Since God had forgiven her and she had forgiven herself, she had to believe her husband's love was bigger than her mistake. To believe he would not forgive her was to harm him and herself. This would be breaking the law of love.

Her final question was: Should she confess all to her husband?

"No," I replied. "Not now. Wait until you both have grown. Some day you will sit down and talk and laugh together about the mistakes you both made. By that time all the pain will have gone from the experience and only the lessons remain."

So before she left that final day, Mrs. Pollard had been completely restored to health. She was happy and grateful. This was the beginning of her serious study of spiritual laws, in which her husband joined her. For, he confessed to me, he held himself responsible for his wife's broken health. He had a good many fears of his own to overcome and especially the one fear that had sent him out seeking the admiration and approval of a younger woman. Together they learned to obey that highest of the spiritual laws—love. Eventually they achieved that status of well being which I tell my students is to "join the happy throng."

It will help us to look a bit further into Mrs. Pollard's case. First, we see that she was suffering from a three-phase fear.

1. Fear of what would happen to her physical body, and to her life itself.

2. Fear of loss of Divine love, loss of respect of her husband and loss of her own self-respect.

3. Fear of loss of liberty or freedom, by being blind and helpless in sickness.

That is quite a load of fear for it includes the three basic fears of man. Out of these fears of threats to the body, mind and spirit, grow thousands of lesser, everyday fears, worries, tensions and anxieties. Small wonder that Mrs. Pollard was sick with fear.

"But that was a most unusual case," someone may say.

"Not at all," I must reply.

For example:

Arnold A. Hutschnecker, M.D., in his book, *The Will to Live,* says that the doctors do not know what is wrong with fully thirty to fifty per cent of the people who come to them. He says that even so the patient is really sick and he gives cases to prove his point. His book was published about ten years ago. Have conditions changed since then? Yes. They have grown worse. For at a recent meeting of medical men it was announced that seventy per cent of those who go to doctors have "no known organic trouble, no sickness at all which medical science can find, but nevertheless these patients are truly sick. Medically, little or nothing can be done for them. . . . The best the doctor can do is to help them understand the cause and source of their problems."

That is what Mrs. Pollard finally understood—the cause and source of her problem and, having neutralized all her fears, she was healed.

A surgeon who takes care of patients in a Veterans hospital recently reported at a medical meeting that "a very large percentage of those admitted for surgery were found to be suffering only from fear."

Here in Pasadena, Dr. John F. Thie, D.C., who is known for outstanding success in manipulation, told me fear if unchecked can result in heart troubles. The fear, he explained, can bring on muscle spasms which first register as heart trouble. He told me of instances where anxiety, prolonged worry and tensions, all of which are forms of fear, affected the very bones of the patient. And I once worked with a young woman who said she knew the very hour the trouble with her leg bones began—because of a fear which was accompanied by revulsion where once there had been respect and love.

The findings of modern science—especially in the fields of psychology, psychiatry and psychosomatic medicine—show us the tragic results of fear as it takes toll of the body, mind and spirit of man. These findings lately include the fact that "Fear is even more contagious than the most communicable disease," and that we often are victims of the "fears of others around us." But science does not tell us much about how those fears of others around us originated, and less still of how to protect ourselves from them. For such understanding and help, we must turn to religion. That is where the Pollards began.

As we proceed with our work here together we shall learn many things the Pollards learned. But here, we can present a few points:

1. God does not punish us for our sins. *We are punished by them.*

2. God is a God of all love, all wisdom and all power.

3. Fear is the result of a false belief that evil can overcome good.

4. By learning to work with the spiritual laws we learn to control the conditions in our lives. We thus prevent fear before it can arise.

If your problem is ill health I respectfully suggest that you wait until you have read through this book before you start to analyze your problem and so overcome fears that may be giving rise to the trouble. There are nine steps to be taken in overcoming fear. We have studied only the first three. We shall take up the fourth in another chapter.

We can take a quick review of those first three steps:

1. *Analyze your problem* for possible hidden fears.

2. *Analyze the fear you find,* or already know you have until you uncover the false belief that gave rise to it. The four are listed in this chapter.

3. *Find new information,* facts which you understand and accept that will set you free from fear.

This we shall be doing throughout the book. Material will be found in our next chapter.

2

Overcoming Fears Concerning Money, Security and Prosperity

Fear can keep you broke, in debt and desperate . . . money grows on trees . . . abundance is the law of nature . . . faith makes dollars and sense . . . plant seeds of faith to grow a crop of prosperity.

STORY FROM LIFE:
The Man Who Thought He Was a Grasshopper

> "Prove me now herewith, if I will not open you the windows of heaven, and pour you out a blessing, that there shall not be room enough to receive it." MALACHI 3:10

The word "security" and the ideas behind it have been hammered into the consciousness of moderns from many angles. Insecurity has become synonymous with fear and dread of the future. Psychologically, a belief in a God of love and fear of the future are incompatible ideas. But many who think of themselves as good Christians unconsciously follow the Communist line when it comes to fear of their future. For example, let me tell

MONEY, SECURITY AND PROSPERITY 19

you about *the young man who thought he was a grasshopper.*

We can call him Jim Barrow and his wife Jane.

"We love each other," said Jane in telling me their story. "But we quarrel more and more about money. Jim says I'm money mad because I want a larger home with separate rooms for our two children and another car for my use. He is so filled with fear that he wants us to pinch every penny twice before we spend it even for grim necessities. He wants to save for a rainy day. But I want to live in the sunny days of right now!"

All fear springs from a false belief about life or the nature of things.

So when we got into the matter of their religious beliefs the root of the Barrows' disagreements was bared. Jane had been brought up in the New Thought Christian religion. Jim had been born into a family whose religious beliefs were based on a God of vengeance, fears of a personal devil and eternal punishment. Jane had joined Jim's church which they still attended but she felt she couldn't take Jim's attitude about money and his fears of the future much longer. A crisis had arisen—Jim was threatened with loss of his job.

The result of our afternoon's conference was that Jim came to see me the following night. He was a clean-cut young man, and very likable. It was obvious he loved his wife and children more than anything else in the world. "I'd sure like to give them everything," he said. "But money doesn't grow on bushes."

"No, it grows on trees," I said.

Taking advantage of Jim's puzzled silence I explained:

"The Bible tells us there were two trees in the Garden of Eden; the tree of life and the tree of death. Money grows on the tree of life. For this tree represents a belief in all good as to God and the Universe and the eventual outcome of man. Poverty, sickness, unhappiness, every unwanted condition grows on the tree of death which is a belief in good *and* evil. A tree represents man's heart or consciousness, what he believes about God, and so, about all life. Thus we are told to keep our heart with all diligence for out of it do come the issues of life. This is necessary because all power is law-locked. The creative power must follow the law of correspondence and so what we *believe* we *receive,* just as Jesus taught. The Garden of Eden story tells us how fear began in the heart of man and the rest of the Bible is devoted to telling us how to overcome fear. And so, Jim, if you want to give your wife and children the good things of life you must eat of the tree of life. To eat means to accept and live certain ideas which the Bible clearly sets forth."

Jim listened in tense silence, his keen blue eyes asking questions of me. Then he said, "O.K. If you know something good and helpful that I don't know, I'll be eternally grateful to hear about it."

That of course was the kind of attitude that led John Wesley upward in consciousness and to founding the

MONEY, SECURITY AND PROSPERITY 21

Methodist Church. Being a life-long Methodist myself, I just had to love Jim for his willingness to learn. Also, being a Methodist, I must witness or die.

"You are a truly meek person," I told Jim. "For to be meek means to be teachable. It is my observation that when God finds a really teachable man He uses him for great purposes as a channel for good. A teachable man can overcome all his fears. How many fears do you have at the moment?"

"Just one," Jim replied. "Fear of losing my job. There is talk at the plant of closing the department where I have worked ever since we were married. If it does close, I'll be out of course."

"What will happen if you lose your job?" I asked.

"I'd lose everything else, too, if I didn't get another in a hurry. No job, no house payments, no car payments, no insurance payments, no back bill payments. We never have going money for more than thirty days ahead. That's why I insist we have to save for a rainy day."

"Aren't you afraid you'd lose prestige with people you know if you lose your job, car, home? What about your wife's love and respect? What would your children, members of your church think of you? Aren't you afraid that loss of your car might mean you'd not get another job? How many fears do you really have?"

"Enough to clobber me down for good," Jim sighed.

We talked awhile about the three-phrase fear he was carrying around, his "sense of impending danger," to the life, love and liberty of his family and himself. When Jim saw his fears clearly we brought up the subject of prayer.

"I've tried to pray but I don't get any satisfaction from my prayers. My pastor prayed with me. He says perhaps it is the will of God for changes to be made and for us to have less. Pastor's wife prayed with Jane. But Jane does not agree with their views on religion. They seem to think Jane wants to live too high; have too much. Do you think it is the will of God for us to have less?" Jim asked earnestly, anxiously.

"No," I replied. "I think it is the will of God for man to have more and more and more. I think God is working out a plan here on earth with human beings. He created us and loaded us with built-in desires which we cannot get rid of and which cry out for fulfillment. Somehow, by our working with our body, mind and spirit to try to fulfill our desires to stay alive, experience love and expand our freedom, we learn, express ourselves in art, music and beauty, search for truth and worship the Creator. By this method of trying to acquire something bigger, something better, something more, we have explored the earth, our own thoughts, civilized ourselves, founded science, religion and philosophy. I think it is a combination of laziness, shifting the blame and burden on God, of ignorance and ungrounded fear to say the will of God is for us to have less. How could it be? God gave us free will. We can refuse to cooperate with His plan. But to limit ourselves is to limit God. To limit God

MONEY, SECURITY AND PROSPERITY 23

and ourselves is also to limit our fellow men. I believe such limitation is a sin; a mistake. It is a proven fact that abundance is the law of nature. God put his created being, man, into an unfinished world. He commanded man to "be fruitful and multiply." This cannot mean simply to beget children. Without discovering more and better ways for food supplies begetting children would be sinful. I believe God intends for us to create more and more good. The raw materials already abound in nature. Ideas for growth may be obtained from God for the asking and being willing to work with them. To refuse to increase is to fail to cooperate with God's purpose.

Since Jim was not lazy, had no intention of shifting a burden or duty he saw to be his own, and was not ignorant in the accepted sense of education and training, his problem clearly was one of ungrounded fear and lack of a plan of procedure for expansion and growth. After several conferences with him going over what he really believed about God, man and their relationship, I said, "Jim, you have been breaking the first commandment all your life."

I had to prove my every point by the Bible, book, chapter and verse. But before we were through Jim saw that he had indeed, *always believed that there was a power greater than God.*

Jim's fear of the future was a fear of an evil able to overcome God, or good. He called that evil power "bad luck," or "company policy," or simply "circumstances beyond my control." He had quite a list of what stood in the way of his good. *His fears of failure were greater than his faith in God.*

What Jim had to learn:

To put any power, person or thing before God is to break the first commandment. Jim was not putting his faith in God but in a "rainy-day fund." He was not worshiping God. He was failing to believe in God as the highest power of the Universe. This fact he finally saw clearly and it proved a great shock to him. There could be no healing until there was understanding.

While Jim had come to talk about his fear of loss of his job we must notice that it was a deeper, hidden, more important fear that really worried him. He wanted to be sure about God's will for him. For fear of displeasing God is one of our deepest and most painful fears because it concerns our greatest desire: to be, to keep our individual identity forever. To displease God can become a threat to our eternal life Self. Like Jim, few of us stop to analyze our fears. But Jim finally saw that his deepest question was not, "What must I do to be sure of earning a living while on earth?" which he called his problem. His deepest question was, "What must I do to be saved after death?" which gave rise to his fears and all his life had held him back from financial success.

Jim's conflict about his desire to earn the greatest possible amount of money and his desire to be right with God (on the side of Grace, as he said) grew out of that root of all human fear which we must mention repeatedly in a variety of ways until we thoroughly understand it.

MONEY, SECURITY AND PROSPERITY 25

The root fear is a belief that *evil can overcome good* Anything which threatens the fulfillment of our desires for life, love and liberty is to us, evil. Always we must remember, if we had no desires we would have no fears.

In Jim's case the evil rested in his unconscious belief in two sides to God's nature—love and punishment. Also, an unconscious belief that there actually was a power of evil, a devil, separate from God. But most of all, Jim knew nothing of the power of his own word, of the power of prayer as it is used in the Christian New Thought movement in which Jane had been reared. Jane knew very well. This difference was the basis of their personal problems. Jane's knowledge led her to expect more of Jim and of life than they were receiving.

Jim maintained that he no longer believed in eternal hell fire and punishment, but the ideas were deep in his unconscious mind from earliest childhood. His need was to learn new truth that would set him free. This Jim did. He began to fill his mind with truth by learning what he really thought about himself. He got it said as follows:

"I look around at the guys with big Cadillacs, swimming pools, and big salaries to support them and I think of the Bible story which describes me to a T. The one where Moses sent his men out to spy for a future home. They came back and said there were giants in that land and that they were in their own sight as grasshoppers. Well, that's me—a grasshopper," he declared and folded his arms across his chest in an attitude of saying, "That's all I am and there's nothing you or anyone else can do about it."

I told him it was up to him whether he was a grasshopper or a giant, and that it was pretty plain to me that Jane was tired of the grasshopper role because she was so certain in her own mind that he actually was a giant acting like a grasshopper. "Overcome your fears and you will find you are a giant," I said.

It is my belief that to get rid of fear on earth is to be rid of it throughout eternity. I believe earth is a school where we learn how to use our God-given powers to fulfill our God-given desires. The reward of learning how to live without fear, how to fulfill our desires, is to find that life really is a heaven on earth. This is the reentering of paradise or the state of perfection, harmonious living in body, mind and spirit which man always dreams about and which is predicted in the Bible as man's eventual accomplishment.

In looking at today's worldwide problems and fears it will help us with our individual fears to remember that this desire for and promise of ultimate perfection, written in man's heart, is what is back of even his wildest Utopian dreams and plans for a better world. But never can it be accomplished by edict of laws of the land, arms, and firepower, by threat and force. It can be done only by the individual working with his own Soul. Soul growth is and ever must be a do-it-yourself job. That is what Jane and Jim set out to do.

I believe in the written program as an aid to changing one's life. The Barrows wrote down a list of things as

MONEY, SECURITY AND PROSPERITY

they were in their lives, including thoughts and fear patterns, which they did not want. Another list was made of things as they desired them to be.

Jim was then earning three hundred dollars a month. I suggested he demand of himself the ability to earn twice that amount, or six hundred dollars a month. (A dollar bought more then than it does today.) A growing family needs an expanding income. They were to remember that God knows what we need before we ask, but we still must ask. The growing consciousness of man needs to expand for more and more freedom. To achieve these two desires would enable them to express more love to each other, their fellow men and to God.

Jane was encouraged to desire, plan and ask for good household equipment. "Every labor-saving appliance is a step toward greater freedom," I told her. "And it will give you more time with the children, for study, for practicing creative prayer and Soul growth."

(Here I sadly admit that for many the time saved with modern conveniences often is merely spent and not invested in Soul growth as it should be. This leads to boredom, frustration and delinquency on every hand. Hence the Soul defeats its own purpose for man was made to grow, forever.)

The Barrows made a "big bold list" of what they desired. They added to it as their courage increased. Soon they agreed on a larger home with a swimming pool. Jim made astonishing progress from the first for now he had his heart right with God. He saw clearly that it was his duty to earn as much as he could and to give as much as he could. They used the following daily affirmation:

The all-providing Mind of God is our real resource and our prosperity and success are assured.

Jim stopped thinking of himself as a grasshopper. He began to see that God has given every man the power to become a giant of accomplishment. He soon bought the second used car for Jane. This gave her new freedom and lifted her spirits. It also took a load off Jim's time. He didn't have to take the children to school, or go for the groceries. Freedom can become capital. Jim was led to go to night school; to take public speaking. He accepted lecture dates. I advised him to have aptitude tests made, to learn whether he was in the right job. He changed jobs after learning his highest natural abilities and got an increase in salary. Jim and Jane worked as a unit and so the power was multiplied through them, under the law of "two agreed."

They left Jim's church and joined a New Thought church where, they reported to me, they "met people of very high faith and consciousness; nobody talks about sickness or bad luck." They made new friends. Their quarrels about money ceased from the start of their project. There was now no fear between them and so no need for anger as a defense against fear. They were happier than they ever had been. "It is an intelligent, understood happiness," Jim enthused. Whenever a desire or problem arose they talked to each other asking, "Is

MONEY, SECURITY AND PROSPERITY 29

it good? Will it help all concerned? Is this an impulse of fear or of faith?" Together they learned.

When a problem arose that frightened them they said, "This is not bigger than God. There is *nothing* bigger than God!" The old and often mentioned slogan, "God is my partner," was very real to them. Day by day their faith grew and their fears diminished. Since the law of correspondence never sleeps, the more they desired and *pictured themselves as receiving* the more they did receive. A circle of success was thus set up, for the more they received the more their faith increased.

Then one day Jane came saying they had an opportunity to buy a fine big home. "Almost half an acre of land," Jane said, her eyes bright with the wonder of it. One of the executives at the plant where Jim then worked was being transferred out of the state. "If they could sell everything at once, without advertising, getting an agent, wasting time, they'd give us a real deal," said Jane. "We are praying for their good just as much as for our own. It's our dream home—rambling ranch style, complete with swimming pool, first and second trust deeds, five bedrooms and three baths! They even want to sell the furniture, wall-to-wall carpets, electrical appliances, everything!"

"Sounds like an answer to your prayer," I agreed.

Jim came that night. We three realized that they already had received the home long before in *idea form*. (For complete understanding of this principle the reader will be helped by my book, *How to Use the Power of*

Your Word.) We did not pray with the thought that God was a Super Man somewhere up in the skies who might withhold this good or might decide to bestow it. We prayed, giving thanks for the power God has given man to work with the Creative power that God used to create planets and man. We had an absolute faith that everything necessary to be done would be done in order for them to acquire that home.

And they did acquire it.

They have continued in their program of more and more of livingness, of love and ever-expanding liberty. They know beyond doubt that this is a way of worshiping God. The windows of heaven have been opened for them. They have learned this great truth about life: the more you give the more you will receive. Success is a circle. They give time, attention, energy, prayer, thought, love and money. As more money comes to them they give more and more to help others to express more of life, love and liberty. We cannot remember it too often: Good travels in a circle. For the Barrows and all others who know how to use their power it is an ever-expanding circle.

If your fears have to do with money, security and prosperity I respectfully suggest that you wait until you have finished the entire book before you set up a program such as the Barrows used. The following will help you now and you can come back to these points later when you are ready for your own prosperity project.

1. *Fear is a habit, a way of looking at life.*

Psychology teaches us we cannot break a habit by working at the habit. That digs it in deeper. We break an old, unwanted habit by replacing it with a new one. We need to create new patterns of thinking. These will create new habits of acting.

2. *Overcome evil with good.*

The Bible tells us we have the power within ourselves to do this. Evil means: "Anything impairing happiness or welfare; affliction; misfortune; opposed to good," says Webster. By thinking of and expecting our desired good we set in motion the power which brings it to us.

3. *Make new demands upon yourself.*

It is not necessary to deny others, to steal or rob or cheat or lie in order to become wealthy. Wealth comes from new ideas that create new goods and services, that give pleasure and comfort and profit to others. Ideas are from God. We get them by making new demands upon ourselves as channels and producers. Psychologists tell us we use only about 10 per cent of our abilities and powers. The law is, a big demand (upon ourselves) brings a big supply from God.

4. *Bless what you have.*

Praise and thanksgiving have power to increase. Use that power.

5. *Love the good of life.*

Some people pretend to despise money and the better things of life. This is denying the goodness of God. To love God is to love good and to love good is to attract it to us through the law of cause and effect, and the law of correspondence. Knowing this, we need never fear for the morrow.

6. *Feel worthy of prosperity and plenty.*

God makes His rain to fall on rich and poor, good and evil alike. God withholds good from no man. Man must develop to the point of his individual awareness of his powers and the laws under which these powers work. God sets no limit to what a man may acquire.

7. *Be a profitable servant.*

In the parable of the talents, Jesus tell us clearly that those who multiplied their talents (which was a measure of money) were given greater good and authority. But the man who was afraid and buried his talent and did not multiply it by putting it to work, was rebuked and that which he had was taken from him and given to the man who now had ten talents as a result of his work.

8. *Do not fear great wealth.*

There is no harm in accumulating great wealth, nor in using great wealth. Just be sure not to let it use you. Some of the greatest blessings that have come to man have come through accumulated wealth, from foundations, research organizations, schools, hospitals, and so forth, which were set up for the giving of more life, love and liberty to the individual and so, the world.

9. *See for yourself the good you desire.*

See yourself *possessing* any desired thing, or condition. And enjoying it. If it is a new hi-fi set, *hear* it as well as see it. If it is a new home, see yourself in it, walking through the rooms. See the colors, fabrics, furniture you want. This practice will help you tremendously to get rid of fear. The battle ever is to think of what you do desire and never to let anything enter your mind that you do not want in your body, mind and affairs. Edison said he owed his success in inventing to the fact that he thought in pictures and not in words. Steinmetz said the same thing.

10. *Tithing is a law of expanding prosperity.*

If you tithe in fear it will not bring back prosperity. You can go broke tithing in fear. The law of cause and effect will create wealth or poverty for you in accordance with your own belief, your feelings, your fears or your faith. It is therefore necessary to be happy, fearless, sure of the future, giving gladly if tithing is to increase your good until there is not room enough to hold it.

11. *Ask for more.*

Go to sleep every night saying, "I am working for God and God is working for me." If God were not working for you, you wouldn't have life or beingness. Ask for more and more and more. Not just of money or wealth. But of wisdom, love, all good.

12. *Keep your mind on God.*

There is not enough money in all the world to make you feel secure. Nothing less than a faith in God, as all love, all wisdom and all power plus your own ability to work directly with Him and for people can give you a sense of security. All things may be wiped out including our planet earth, but our Soul and God stand, forever.

13. *Good desires are from God.*

Nothing can keep your good from you but yourself. You need nothing more than your powers of desire, decision, asking, prayer, love, faith and work to create wealth. As long as there are hungry children in the world poverty is an evil. Don't fear poverty. Overcome it.

14. *Keep in touch with the expansion ideas of the best minds of our time.*

This keeps you tuned in with the truth that abundance is the law of nature. For example:

General David Sarnoff, chairman of the Radio Corporation of America, recently said of tomorrow's wealth "I think . . . we will find more wealth in space than we have found beneath the surface of the ground."

Fresh water is a form of wealth. In dry California we are ever aware of that fact. It now seems possible to turn ocean water into fresh water at a cost of about twenty cents per thousand gallons. An old, old dream of man to make the desert blossom as the rose, will yet come true.

For the first time in history there is hope of food, clothing, shelter, health and education for all. It will not come overnight. There is much growing to be done on the part of those destined to receive. But man is now working out of the poverty, out of the fear consciousness which have hovered over the world since civilization began.

A few days ago Allyn B. Hazard told the Aeronautics Seminar held at Caltech, in Pasadena, that close to one hundred persons will take a moon trip by 1970. This staff specialist for the Space-General Corporation also said that 100,000 people will journey to the moon by the year 2000. Progress in space travel is so rapid that Hazard and others are constantly revising their figures of how far, how soon. The movement is always toward less time and greater space.

3

Overcoming Fears Concerning Love, Marriage and Other Human Relations Problems

The secret of successful love is to love without fear . . . love is a twelve-sided affair . . . to love is to know God . . . let not your heart be troubled . . . live with a purpose.

STORY FROM LIFE:
The Woman Who Gorged Herself on Apples of Fear

> "There is no fear in love; but perfect love casteth out fear: because fear hath torment. He that feareth is not made perfect in love. We love him, because he first loved us."
>
> ST. JOHN 4:18–19

A few years ago while I was lecturing on how to overcome fear a most unusual thing happened. As I talked about the Garden of Eden story, I noticed an attractive, well-dressed lady sitting in the front row, only a few feet from where I stood, nodding her head in agreement as I made point after point. She seemed to be completely oblivious to her surroundings, listening with rapt attention, which was very flattering to me as the speaker. As I continued she entered more deeply into the spirit of my talk, leaning forward on her chair with her mouth slightly open. Having explained that the tree of knowledge of good *and* evil is the tree of death because the fruit of such a belief is fear, I said:

"If we are not careful we will often eat apples of fear and then wonder why we have so many tummy aches in life."

At that point the lady arose and with great feeling and a refreshing abandon, cried out, "That's me all over, sister!"

It nearly broke up our meeting, though I was sure at the time that everyone there admired her as much as I did. Later, the lady—I like to think of her as Edna Rigger—came to my hotel to apologize for interrupting me. I assured her I was not annoyed, but pleased and proud of her. She had the look of the American pioneer woman, her feet solidly on the ground and an uncompromising determination in her honest blue eyes. But also, she obviously was deeply troubled.

"What have you found that is bigger than God?" I asked.

"Look," she replied, handing me a colored post-card picture of the Sir Joseph Hooker Oak, which stands in Bidwell Park, in Chico, California. "My tree of good and evil is as big as this tree and full of fruit! I'm blood sister to Eve," said Edna. "I just gorge myself on those apples of fear. How can I destroy the root of such a big tree with the amount of faith I have? It would be like trying to dig out Hooker Oak with a penknife. That's the size of my faith—penknife size."

I studied the card and read the description of that famous landmark and learned the oak was then estimated to be more than a thousand years old; that it rose to more than one hundred feet in the air and had a trunk circumference of almost thirty feet. Its branches spread over an area of one hundred and fifty feet in diameter.

"I hope your tree of fear is not that big," I said.

"Bigger," Edna assured me. "And if you count every leaf on that tree as one of the fruits of fear I have been eating all my life you'll get a picture of how things are with me and my family. How can I destroy my tree of fear with my little old penknife faith?"

"By learning new truths and living them," I said. "By getting a purpose in life so big and so important that it will overcome fear. You can walk away from the tree and go eat of the tree of life. What is your greatest fear of the moment?" I asked.

"Something wrong with my youngest child, Billy Boy. Few weeks ago he began to cry at the breakfast table. We asked him what was wrong. He said, 'I don't want to grow up. There are too many bad things to happen to people.' I took him to the doctor who said there was nothing wrong with him except too many horror movies on Saturday and being batted to pieces by our crazy home life.

LOVE, MARRIAGE, HUMAN RELATIONS

Billy is sensitive. Doctor said he needed an awful lot of love. That's when I decided I had to learn something. *Things have got to change!*" she declared so firmly that I knew she would follow through on a self-help program and agreed to try to help her.

Thus began our work together, carried on by mail later. Edna's written story of her life opened as follows:

"I was conceived in fear and borne in dread, neither needed, wanted nor loved as a child. There were so many of us little brats that life was too much for poor mother and she was an invalid most of the time. Father was an alcoholic when he was out of jail. We lived on hand-me-downs and grudged money."

Edna included her fears of growing up, struggling for a modest education, the jobs she held, the people in her life and her "big deep plunge" into marriage.

"I think we love each other," Edna wrote, "but to this day I am uncomfortable in Rodney's presence and especially if his parents or college friends are with us. He then says and does things that hurt me and make me feel like a country clod which I guess I am."

Edna's husband, Rodney, was a college man, and a registered pharmacist. They had four children aged six to sixteen. Edna gave me vivid word pictures of her problems. Her husband was too critical of her and the children. The children quarreled with one another. Two years before, their combined fears of the future and rising living costs, had driven Edna from home into the commercial world. "I think my husband has been angry every hour since," she wrote. Associates where she worked were problem people. A good many of them got in her hair. Her story ended with:

"We are good people, pay our bills, don't drink or smoke or gamble. We don't steal or lie or cheat on each other and we go to church on Easter, Christmas and Mother's Day. On the surface we are an average happy family, but the truth is our home life is just plain hell!"

"You can remodel your home life from hell, which is inharmony, into a heaven of happiness and harmony" I told her.

Edna was willing to try. "But please give me something to read and follow," she requested, "something that will make me stop and think which tree I am eating from, and in time."

From her report to me Edna's case looked like this:

1. *Her problem* was unhappiness in the family. She felt they were all drifting with no purpose in life but just to live from day to day. The two older children were almost out of hand and straining to get out of the unpleasant home.

2. *Edna's fears were:* Things would always be this way or worse; that she was powerless to change them; the situation was hopeless; no help to be had.

3. *Her basic false belief* about life which gave rise to the fears was that God exists, but man cannot know Him or contact Him. There was no help to be had from prayer; if no help now, then none later, after death. While that part was subconscious it had its effect in her daily life.

She feared she was missing her only chance of happiness. She feared she was not a very good wife or mother.

4. *The results* of Edna's false basic belief and fears were that she felt unloved, that life was "just too hard," and not worth the living.

The crisis that drove Edna to seek help and to hope there was help to be had, was hearing her child voice her own often secretly held thought: life is not worth living. And, as I told her, without God's love for man, without God's plan for man, without the privilege and power of prayer, without love given and received, life indeed would not be worth living.

Edna's problems with her husband, children, other people at work, and in-laws all had to do with love. Edna had a tremendous capacity for love and wanted to express it fully and to receive it fully. That was her nature. This urge of her nature was in conflict with her belief about God and so, all life, including her husband and children and herself. She was afraid to love fully for fear of rejection and often felt there was rejection when there was not. Thus her fears set up repressed angers. Repressed anger can completely destroy married happiness and sex life. Also, Edna's unhappy memories of childhood often stood in the way of her present living.

"You are a very strong character, a potential leader," I told Edna. "Your family will believe as you do. You must learn to love fully, without any fear whatever. Remember, all those silent angers are defenses against fear. You must learn to love without fear."

Edna set out to change the conditions from what they were to what she wanted them to be. Her goal: a happy, fear-free home life. Always we must start right where we are with what we have. Instead of waiting for lessons and further learning, Edna set to work at once with my first suggestion. Mealtimes had been noisy, unhappy affairs filled with tension that frequently exploded into temper tantrums. Edna had come to dread them. I advised her to invite the Spirit of Love to be her guest one evening. I told her the names of some of the children of love are Courtesy, Kindness, Patience, and Calmness.

Edna set an extra plate at the table that night. The children wanted to know "Why do we have to have someone tonight, Mom?" Each had something he wanted to talk over with her. Her husband growled, "Well, I hope she's on time. I'm hungry."

"Our guest is already here," said Edna. "And she will not mind if we all just plow in and eat and grunt like pigs and quarrel and bicker. Our unseen guest here is the Spirit of Love."

Her words were greeted with embarrassment at first. Then Edna said, "While the roast gets another ten minutes, I want you all to be quiet while I read to you." She then read Paul's words on love.

I hope the reader will turn to his Bible and read the entire thirteenth chapter of First Corinthians, the most inspiring words about love ever put into language. It begins:

"Though I speak with the tongues of men and of angels,

and have not charity (love), I am become as sounding brass, or a tinkling cymbal."

"We could do with less brass and more of love around here," said Edna as she put the Bible down.

In the quiet that followed Edna announced that after dinner she wanted all of them to write out a list of what they'd like to have changed in their family life; what each one feared most. Her idea was accepted with interest. All during dinner Edna kept the children quiet by lifting a forefinger to her mouth, and looking at the offending one she then pointed toward the vacant seat where sat the invisible Spirit of Love.

Afterward her husband said, "That dinner without brass was the most peaceful meal we've had in a long time. I sure appreciate it."

After dinner the children wrote out their fears and what they wanted changed. Billy Boy's fear was that "every time Mommy goes to work I'm afraid she will not come back again."

The teen-agers were afraid to bring friends home. The pre-teen was afraid he would never make good in school. Edna's husband feared he never could earn enough money to give Edna and the children all he wanted them to have, which surprised and pleased Edna. "But I didn't let him know I was pleased," she said. Edna had for so long held back her natural impulses of love expressions that she often withheld praise and encouragement that needed to be given. Fear of rejection, or of not being understood kept her silent.

"To withhold praise and expressions of love where needed and deserved can be cruelty," I told Edna. "No one ever received too much love."

Some of the points of truth Edna learned and put to use were:

Practicing the awareness of God's love.

This was done by working with her children. "You do your best for them because you love them and because you are by nature a love person," I said. "Where did the love in your heart come from? If it did not come from God, Creator, giver of life, then where did you get it? Take time to think about your joy in giving and doing for your family for this takes you back to God, the source of love."

Love is a growing part of the human Soul.

Edna learned that love is a growing part of the human Soul and that not much was heard of love before the coming of Christ. In the Old Testament we learn there were 614 rules in the Pentateuch which were broken on pain of punishment. Moses caught a man picking up sticks on the Sabbath and he was taken outside the city gates and stoned to death. That is as far as understanding of God's nature and laws had developed at that time with those people.

But, as time went on, and the Soul of man, the individual and so the race, developed we find man's ideas of love increasing. In the fifteenth Psalm we find those rigid 614 rules reduced to eleven. Eventually in the Prophets we find them reduced to three: "Do justly, love mercy, and walk humbly with thy God." Finally came Jesus the Christ who reduced all the laws to one: *the law of love.*

Of all the fears which beset humanity none is more painful than those having to do with love, for love is a twelve-sided affair and we deal with it in some way every hour of our lives. Since we are all born hungry for love it will help us to overcome all our fears to understand the needs of love. Let us take a look at those twelve sides of love:

In group one we need status with God which has four parts as follows:

1. We need to know God loves us.

2. We need to love God with happiness, praise and gratitude.

3. We need to know God accepts our love, even when we do wrong.

4. We need to know we are worthy of God's love even when we do wrong deliberately or make mistakes ignorantly.

In group two we need status with other people:

1. We need to know others love us; to feel acceptable.

2. We need to know we are worthy of the love of others.

3. We need to love others; to value them.

4. We need to have others value us and accept our love.

In group three we need status with Self:

1. We need to be a lovable person, a Self, good company alone.

2. We need to know we are upright, have a clear conscience.

3. We need to be satisfied that we are doing somewhere near our best in life, making a worth while contribution.

4. We need to love ourselves even when we fail utterly, or fall short of our high ideals and objectives and regardless of what others may or may not think of us and what we believe God expects of us.

Edna needed to know all the twelve sides of love. For the child who feels he is not loved, wanted or needed is a problem child. He will remain a problem person all his life until he satisfies at least some of his total hunger for love. Not to have love gives him nameless fears all his life. I have worked with men and women past sixty-five years of age who were still seeking some of the needs of love that never had been met.

Edna could not at first believe that her husband also had fears and needed a great deal of encouragement, love and praise from her. I told her, "Love is a woman's work. Don't slight it, ever." And when she began to "take the initiative and tell Rodney I loved him and to become interested in his work and problems, I found he did need and appreciate my help. I decided I would not wait for him to say he loved me. I would just take that for granted. I could say I loved him, and say it first. It has paid off handsomely," she wrote. "And now we talk everything over and my silent angers have all gone."

Soon after her studies began Edna decided they could get along without her "working-for-money job" and an-

LOVE, MARRIAGE, HUMAN RELATIONS 47

nounced she would stay home and do a better job there. The whole family improved from the first day.

Edna found it difficult to believe she was an attractive woman. I had her stand in front of her mirror every day and say: "Wonderful, beautiful, precious you!" It helped her a great deal. She eventually could evaluate her good qualities and accepted the fact that she was a success as a woman.

As Edna changed her opinion of herself, she discovered her husband showed a new respect and admiration for her. *The charming person is one who is not afraid of tomorrow; and who has a faith he can rely on in any situation in life.* Edna's self-respect went on to feeling worthy of God's love, to love of others as well as of her family. She became a charming and poised person. Living and loving without fear she "began to enjoy being married and being a wife and to feel she really was making the grade at last."

Edna found that by being home they cut the doctor bills to almost nothing. She stopped eating out so much. "We had been running away from our unhappy home life," she said. They never missed her salary. "Rodney is happier than he ever has been in our married life," she wrote joyfully.

Edna put up a hand-made placard in the dining room which read: Love Is the Head of This House. When one of the children misbehaved she would say, "The Head of the House is watching you," and the child would quiet down. When she felt fear or resentment toward her husband she remembered "the head of the House."

As time went on Edna solved problems as they arose by saying to herself and teaching her family:

Through love, God created man to have a Being in His own image and likeness to love, to watch over and to help to develop toward some goal we do not yet understand. But it is good. Since God's love was big enough to create man it is big enough to care for all of us right now. But Edna, being the wonderful direct and forceful love person that she was, finally cut the idea to one sentence. She would hold in her mind the fact that there is nothing bigger than God's love for His children. She would say aloud to herself or family, "There's *nothing* bigger than God!" without ever discussing the problem. It became a family byword.

Edna wrote: "Every time I forget and start to fear evil, the whole family reacts. Life says to me, you name it Edna, and I'll bring it."

That is what it says to all of us, and has been saying to man since the dawn of civilization, or the coming of man's free will.

Many times Edna wrote, "I slipped again, but I'll never give up." She had come to realize that the good we desire today has an eternal value for us. Her husband joined a church with her "after he saw how much good it was doing the children and me," she wrote. And he eventually went into business for himself because Edna, who had learned to take the initiative, first saw the way and he happily followed her ideas. Today they own a prosperous drugstore business. My last letter from them said "We still belong to the happy throng." It was signed with their name and "Dwellers in Paradise."

If your problem has to do with love you will find much help in the succeeding chapters. Meantime here are several points:

1. You are not alone, not unloved. God had need of you or you would not be here. Fulfill that need and love will come and fear will go.

2. What we call evil is a wrong use of our good, God-given power. God our Creator continues to create through us his offspring. We create at a low general level, every time we think. We create at a higher level when we picture what we desire. We create at the highest level when we picture with a purpose and speak the word for it. It is because we do have this power that we need have no fear of anything outside of ourselves.

Step four in overcoming fear is: *set a purpose in life*.

Be sure to set one that is of tremendous importance to you. Let it mean almost as much as life itself. Work under love at that purpose and no fear can touch you. This was what Edna Rigger did as we have seen in this chapter.

Also: remember to keep up with the world picture of love at work. World fear goes as worldwide love comes in. A recent scientific discovery sets the date of man on earth at 1,750,000 years. We can be pretty certain that fear of one human being for another is also that old. We will stop our wars, murders, hatreds and suspicions when enough people understand themselves and their neighbors and God. Only then can they conduct their affairs of life within the golden rule so that we can have worldwide, permanent peace, plenty, happiness and freedom from fear. Thousands of efforts are being made on this front. For example:

1. The exchange student program is now so well established that it probably will continue for generations until the peoples of one country know a great deal about those of another. As walls of ignorance are broken down, fear and suspicion go and love comes in.

2. We now have 200,000,000 Christians in the world. The number is growing rapidly. This is most hopeful for a world free of fear. For "Where the Spirit of the Lord is, there is liberty." (II Corinthians 3:17 R.S.V.)

3. Dr. Ernest M. Ligon, Director of Character Research Projects of Union College, recently said: "If even a quarter of the money spent during the last decade on luxurious church school buildings had been invested in research, the dividends in terms of the fruits of faith, would have been a hundredfold greater. The awakening urge for research in religious education, which is being seen on every hand, must be nourished and made to grow into the force it can become."

Everywhere we look, intelligent men and women are at work to help people to understand people. For when understanding comes, fear goes. But we must always come back to ourselves and see that we overcome our own fears. Until we do the fearless world around us will not help us much. So let us go on with our lessons.

4

Overcoming Fears Concerning Liberty and Freedom

"Liberty or death" is a necessary law of life and Soul growth . . . you will never be free from bondage or domination of others until you are free from fear . . . only you can break the chains that bind you . . . freedom under God is all good . . . you were born to be free . . . put your free will to work to gain the knowledge, experience and self-expression you desire.

STORY FROM LIFE:
The Man Who Lived in a Cage

> *"I am come that they might have life, and that they might have it more abundantly."*
> ST. JOHN 10:10

If we could get rid of all degrees of fear, including anxiety, worry, depression and groundless sense of guilt, we would no longer need anger, hatred, violence, wars and punishment which are defenses against fear. If we could eliminate all fear from the human mind we would pretty well do away with the practice of lying, stealing, cheating, trespassing, threats and aggressions. For these are largely the result or, what I call the children, of fear.

Fear drives many people to dominate others in the mistaken belief that it is their duty to do so and good for the soul of the dominated one. But domination is wrong. God gave each man free will and an individual Soul with his desires for expressing his individual Self. Sooner or later the individual will arise and demand his God-given freedom.

For example, let me tell you about *the man who lived in a cage*.

We can call him Paul Deutchler. He was twenty-nine years old, unmarried, an only child whom his parents had dominated all his life. They still talked down to him as to a six-year old.

When Paul first phoned me long distance asking for an appointment I asked, "What is your problem?"

"I am losing my mind," he replied.

We set an appointment date and a few days later he drove up to my home early in the morning. When I met him at the door I realized he was spiritually sick and was about ready to give up trying to solve his problems. These were driving him to the distraction which he called "losing his mind."

Paul was a handsome, big man, six-feet three, with tortured gray eyes, rumpled sandy hair and a shy manner. He had driven all night and had not had breakfast, he said, but refused food. "I just have to talk to you," he said. It was a beautiful summer day with the joy of life,

LIBERTY AND FREEDOM

the presence of God and the warmth of the sun in the air around us. But this was lost on the young man. So I took him to the patio to let him talk.

The patio of my home is at the rear of the house. It faces east, a secluded fenced-in garden away from street noises, and is quiet. Generous in size, it has a brick flooring kept washed in summer for coolness. Enclosed with a wide-angle screen it permits an unobstructed view of Mt. Wilson not far away. There is a comfortable and protected feeling in the patio because of the citrus trees—kumquat, golden Rangpur lime, lemon, orange and tangerine—close by. These trees, always green with blossoms and fruit at various stages of development, give a feeling that all is well. Nature in her loveliest moods and aspects is reassuring to the troubled spirit of man.

Paul stretched his big body in the big wicker chair and looked out over the housetops, beyond the high steeple of the Nazarene church a block away and said, "Nice."

I nodded and waited. Paul sat quiet, looking around the garden. His spirit was visiting with point after point of the scene before him. At the far end of the garden there is a wisteria vine, a tall silver maple tree, pink crape myrtle, a Santa Rosa plum and other shrubs and vines. That morning there were thousands of bougainvillaea blossoms, like rubies in the sun, covering the roof of the garage and the sheds. The wild birds, which we have fed for years, come and go all day long. The ground is left bare for their privilege and purpose. Some were there then, feeding or dusting their feathers, making happy bird sounds. All this might not seem important to the reader. But it was of the greatest importance to the soul of the weary and badly frightened young man. For all together it said to him, "There is peace to be had." I often wish hospitals caring for the mentally ill could work out such a "nature" treatment for their patients. I long have observed the good effect of natural peace, quiet and color on the disturbed person.

Finally Paul spoke again:

"I came hoping you would recommend a good psychiatrist to me," he said.

"Why do you want a psychiatrist?" I asked. (I often do suggest that those who come to see me see a psychiatrist. They are not yet ready for the help I try to give.)

"Because I am tired of living in a cage," he said. "And if I don't find a way out soon I'm afraid of what I might do—"

"What is it that makes you so afraid?" I asked.

Haltingly at first, then in a rush and tumble of words his whole story came out without much prompting on my part. Overly simplified and necessarily made brief it was this:

He was born and all his life had lived in a small town where his father owned a hardware store, the pride and joy of the older man's life. But Paul detested the place. However, he worked there because his father insisted and he "always had minded his father." On a recent morning he had been showing an axe to a customer and suddenly the thought had crossed his mind to kill his father with the axe. It frightened and sickened him so that he had gone to a psychiatrist. But he had not been able to tell him his story. He told him he was tired, felt unhappy, thought he needed to go somewhere else to live. The psychiatrist knew his father. Paul began to feel that the psychiatrist was part of the cage that enclosed him; that he would contact his father. So he drew money from his own account and started driving away from home leaving a letter to his parents that he was going west on a vacation.

Paul had read one of my books which contains a case history of a woman who was healed of mental illness, and so had contacted me.

"What is it about your father that you fear most?" I asked.

"That it will never end. It has been going on all my life. I often planned to break away but mother would cry and dad would shame me and I would feel guilty and ungrateful and stay on. When I was first out of high school it seemed a good thing to do. I never had another job except with my father, never had to worry about getting one. They don't charge me room and board. Dad pays me well."

Paul's religious training was fundamentalist. Hell was right down there and heaven was right up there, and his father Hiram Ezekiel Deutchler, certainly had a reserved seat on the right-hand side of the Lord Jesus Christ—not far removed from dead center where the very best people would sit. Paul's reaction to life showed early training of a multitude of Thou Shalt Nots. His parents were more of the eye for an eye and tooth for a tooth religion of Moses than of the loving, forgiving Jesus Christ and the Grace of God for all sinners beliefs.

"Everything was evil," said Paul. "Fun, parties, cards, dancing, sex. Our neighbor boys would go dancing in the basement of their church but our church held dancing was sin and never permitted it. To kiss a girl or to hold her hand was third-degree rape. Every man was born evil and in sin. As a child I used to fear I might die during the night and wake up in hell."

As a result of the strict training he had left the church entirely in spirit and intent. He attended "now and then to keep Dad from yapping at me about it." But he had no faith in the religion he heard. He had a great deal of scorn instead. Later, when we got into what he liked and his individual nature we found that he was born to question, doubt, argue, disagree and had a fine mind for research, a born skeptic. As a child, his father had slapped him or sent him to his room without supper when he dared to question the rightness of his parents' religious views.

"I early learned not to open my mouth, to play dumb," he said. "But I lived a sort of life of my own through secret reading and doing my own thinking. But I was never sure I was right." He always planned to leave home, to go out on his own. But never had made a move to do so. The crisis had come when out of the blue the idea to kill his father with the axe had flashed across his mind.

"I guess I hate my father," he said brokenly, tears in his voice and eyes. "I wish I didn't. But I do."

LIBERTY AND FREEDOM

We began with the healing thought that hatred is a defense against fear, and that the "caged bird owes no allegiance." His fears were of losing his God-given freedom, of never being free to do the work he had come to earth to do; being denied self-expression and getting accurate answers to his heart's questions. Sitting there that bright morning I told him something like this:

"Like all children of God you came to earth with three great hungers to feed. *First,* hunger for more and more of life itself, leading on to eternal life. *Second,* hunger for perfect love to receive and to give which includes sex, and which leads finally to the eternal love of God. *Third,* hunger for freedom and in the last analysis this is the most important of the three. For just to stay alive and experience perfect love put together are not enough. So God gave us free will. We must have freedom in which to use that free will if our Soul is to grow. And Soul growth, learning how to use our free will under the law of love is the purpose of our being here on earth."

As I talked quietly Paul's face began to show signs of his spirit being freed from some of the tension he long had suffered.

I went on:

"Without this freedom of will there can be no question of morals, no responsibility of man to God. There can be no thought of reward or punishment at the hands of God. Nature, past history, modern science and the Christian religion all teach us the same truth, that man was born for freedom. Since this is a God-given right no man has the right to enslave another. Eventually, man will learn and earn the status of the glorious liberty of the Sons of God. You were born instinctively knowing that. There isn't anything wrong about wanting to be yourself. You have not understood how to go about doing that."

The expression in Paul's face had continued to change. He was keyed up with interest, but he had started to relax from the terrible fear and sense of shame and guilt he had been living with for the past few weeks. When I then suggested that he have breakfast he said it would be welcome. I went into the house to arrange for it to be prepared and served in the patio. When I returned he said to me:

"Oh, thank God, you are not going to hate me or condemn me!"

"Of course not," I replied. "But I hope to show you that you do not really hate your father. You hate yourself for not having broken away from his domination years ago. Your wanting to kill him is a symbol of wanting to kill a weakness, or a fear within yourself which you subconsciously feel you should have overcome years ago. You hate yourself for having tolerated this situation for so long. Your self-hatred is a defense against your own fears that you may never have the courage or strength to make the break. But you do have," I assured him.

After breakfast, which he ate with such relish that I knew he was ready and able to do some more intensive work, we set at it.

The teaching went on about as follows:

"Like all our basic desires, our need for self-expression was implanted in us by God, the Creator. We are individuals. There are no two thumb prints alike, no two snowflakes, not even two blades of grass are alike. Trying to press everyone into one mold is dangerous, contrary to God's law. Father God and Mother Nature so prolific, so creative, never repeat a pattern. Creativity has a tremendous part to play in the scheme of things. God works through each of his creations. We are born individuals, units of being and, I am persuaded, we are to remain so throughout all eternity. To keep our identity, our very own personality is our greatest and most important desire. This is why "Liberty or Death" is a necessary law of life for Soul growth."

"I guess that is what made me decide I had to leave home," Paul said.

"Yes," I agreed. "More peoples in history have migrated away from their homeland in order to be free than for any other reason. To the highly evolved soul, freedom is valued above life itself and rightly so. You need to be free."

"Yes, I see that, now. But how do I do it?"

And then our real work began. All else had been preparation for a starting point.

Paul's basic belief about life (see Chapter 1) was the belief in separation; that God exists, but no help is to be had from Him and no contact can be made with Him. This belief gives rise to the fear of being inadequate to the problems of life, fear of competition and lack of cooperation with other people and of loneliness. Here the evil power resides in others, circumstances, nature. Paul was an example of the fact that his false belief about life often leads to mental illness. His belief almost demanded that he hate the kind of God his father believed in. It also had given him a troubled outlook as a boy and teenager. His parents persuaded him he was better off living with them where they could look after him. Paul never had faced the fact, but he actually thought of himself as sick or "different," and so, as a less person. (See the twelve sides of love in Chapter 3.)

"And that's what I mean by living in a cage," Paul summed up the long recital of his life.

"You have done this to yourself," I reminded him. "You remained in the cage they built around you. *You let it happen.* You used love of your parents as an excuse to stay under their domination. But one of the reasons was that you found it easier to work for your father than to get another job in competition with others. And he paid you well. Your cage was as much of a haven as a prison. You have not married and you say you have no girl friends. We must ask why?"

"Because I don't want to become involved," Paul promptly replied. "A girl might fall in love with me and I don't want to marry. Marriage would mean another cage."

"Wouldn't it also mean responsibilities that you fear might be difficult to meet? That you might not be able to discharge? The trouble with living a protected life,

LIBERTY AND FREEDOM 61

a caged existence, is that we lose our belief that we can take care of ourselves on the outside. Your desire for freedom is in conflict with your desire to be protected. You will have to choose which you want—freedom and responsibility, or live in a cage and be assured bread and care. Have you sold your birthright of freedom for a mess of pottage?" I asked.

Paul thought it over and said, "Yes, I guess I have," and told me of his further fears of people who had power to hurt him or rob him of freedom. They were many and not too well defined. "I just don't want to become involved," he said. It was not from selfishness, which often is the case of the stand-off. He was actually generous and kindhearted. He feared further loss of freedom. When we talked at length about the law of love he started to change some of his old ideas and his fears began to give way.

He had to learn the law of love because his demands for freedom were so great. And freedom outside of love is anarchy. This kind of freedom creates crime, sickness, poverty, all manner of evil and chaos. Paul's need was for harmony, peace and a great deal of "This is the way, walk ye in it," to use his freedom well.

At the end of our first day Paul said he then felt he did not need to see a psychiatrist again. I told him psychiatry, in the main, advises the patient to "adjust," to accept himself as he is and the world as it is and others as they are. But that the Christian religion bids you to expand, to become more and more. I advised him to start to expand his livingness in body, mind and spirit. I advised him to walk, learn to dance, go swimming and learn to play golf. He played the piano better than average and could sing well. I suggested he rent an apartment, a piano and sing and play a great deal. Also, to have aptitude tests made which would help him to understand his nature, abilities and talents.

"I think you are such a doubting Thomas that you could make a career out of it," I told him. "Find out if this is true."

Paul found a new delight in life as he started to expand. His greatest worry was that his parents would "catch up with him and take him home." He wrote them cautious letters without giving an address. He was ready to take a daytime course of study and attended a series of lectures at night, when his parents came to his apartment unannounced. Through his bank checks at home and his automobile license number they had moved heaven and earth and tracked him down, his father gloated proudly.

The parents took charge of Paul, tried to persuade him to go back home with them. "Why did you leave us, son? You were making a good living working in my store," said his father.

"Not a good living, Dad," Paul objected. "Just earning money. Living, no. I've come to think I now have to live my own life in my own way, or die."

"That proves you need to come home with us," said his parents. But Mr. Deutchler's arguments and Mrs. Deutchler's tears failed to move Paul. He phoned me saying,

"They are making me feel like a heel, a sinner, a criminal and worthless, ungrateful son. I am trying hard not to tell Dad about the axe. Will you see them?"

And so they came to see me without Paul.

Mr. Deutchler's attitude as well as his firm words let me know that while he might not always be right, still he never was wrong about a matter. And the matter he was so right about and wanted to convert me to, was the danger of hell fire to which I had subjected his son and was certainly subjecting myself. After some lengthy conversation I said, "But Mr. Deutchler, *why* do you not want to give up the idea of eternal punishment in hell? Why must you believe in hell?"

"Because," he answered in great earnestness and considerable heat, "I know so many people who ought to go there!"

I did not say, "Then you are a greater judge than God? Do you believe an earth parent should punish his child every day this year for something he did last year? Is your desire for a living hell of eternal punishment for others a breaking of the law of love, even at the golden rule level? Does your hope of hell for others dishonor the love and greatness of God?"

I did not say any of it. I just sat there silently reminding myself that Mr. Deutchler was a child of God and that God loved him every bit as much as He loved me. My silence bothered Mr. Deutchler perhaps more than my words could have. He glared at me angrily and said:

"You are *supposed* to be a life-long Methodist, Mrs.

Mann! How is it that you have given up the belief in hell?"

"Because," I replied, "I do not know anyone who ought to go to hell."

My worthy adviser made no comment.

Mrs. Deutchler wanted me to advise her boy to go home where he belonged. "He is sick," she argued.

"What made him sick?" I asked. "He is certainly getting well now. He is going back to school and preparing for a life work that will give him happiness and self-expression."

But she was worried about Paul's morals. She wanted me to know she thought it was very sinful of me to get her son to learn to dance. "Remember, it was a dancing woman who caused John the Baptist to lose his head," she said, her worried eyes accusing me.

"No," I disagreed, "it was not the dancing girl Salome, but her designing and revengeful mother, Herodias; who caused John the Baptist to lose his head. The dutiful daughter but obeyed her domineering mother's command. But your Paul is not about to lose his head. He is about to gain back some of his God-given liberty which he lost by default owing to his not realizing the value of it."

That's about the way our visit went. Paul held his ground and did not return home with his parents. Later he asked why his father so wanted to believe in hell. I explained that Mr. Deutchler's righteousness was actually a fear of punishment. "He is so afraid of punishment at the hands of God that he is afraid he will not hate sin nearly enough. He overcompensates."

"I'm sorry they walked all over you," Paul apologized after his parents' visit which they had duly reported to him in full.

"Why should I mind being walked over?" I asked. "I am a bridge between old and new ideas. A bridge is a connecting pathway between two pieces of land or opposing views. Sometimes the ditch beneath the bridge is wide and deep and dangerous. So let them walk. No one tells me I have to do this work. It is a self-appointed task."

After his parents had gone home Paul began to make great strides in his learning and happiness. One day when he was playing the piano in our home and singing "America" he paused to say, " 'Author of liberty, great God our King'—well that's the kind of God I can respect and love —the author of liberty," and I knew he was safe.

"But remember," I warned him, "unless you choose to use your liberty it will be taken from you by others. It is a law of nature. The body floating idly by will be absorbed, drawn into any powerful force in the vicinity. Your parents are two very powerful people. Stop blaming them. Love them. They did the best they knew how to do."

Paul sold his twelve-year-old car and bought a little foreign-made one. His advance in social skills was remarkable. His work continued at a high level. One day he said, "I think I ought to get married."

"Marriage is a well established and honorable institution," I told him, as we were sitting in the patio one late afternoon, watching the wild birds. Paul had learned a good deal about women and love-making by watching the wild doves in the garden. That day he said, of a particularly ardent male dove, "Look at him knocking himself out." The male dove was coo-coo-cooing and bowing to the seemingly indifferent female who always moved away, but never very far. "He sure means business," said Paul admiringly.

"Yes," I said. "He is not afraid to be caught. Because he knows there is no freedom outside of the law of love. He is courting a mate, promising to help bring up the children. She will have none of him if he is afraid of the responsibilities of family life."

"Do you think he's going to convince her?" Paul asked as the lady dove arose and flew gracefully away, closely followed by the gentleman dove.

"We get a new crop of doves every year," I replied. "So long as we work with nature we find she works with us. Through fear you have been trying to curb your nature most of your life. But I feel that you are now ready to start living fully."

Not long after that Paul made a good and happy marriage and I knew I could take him off my "Please God" list and put him onto my "Thank You, God" list. He has been there ever since.

Some of the points Paul learned are:

1. *The door that leads into a prison also leads out—* the door of thought.

2. *Hunger for knowledge will never die,* but rather in-

LIBERTY AND FREEDOM 67

crease in the Soul of man as time goes on. Our need for self-expression increases as we learn more and more.

3. *When you want freedom badly enough you will get it.*

We are now ready to take the fifth step in overcoming fear, which is: Learn quickly to *trace, place* and *erase* an uneasiness before it becomes a fully developed fear. We do this as follows:

1. When you are conscious of an uneasy feeling, something is not quite right, *trace* it to its rising point. It will have to do with the threat of some desired good. Name it, as need for a better job, or threat of losing an old one.

2. *Place* the developing fear in the *basic urge* group to which it belongs. Remembering always, if we had no desires we would have no fears.

3. Name the basic urge, as for eternal life, name the temporary threat, as, no money to maintain earth life and then *erase* the fear through reasoning. For example, as Edna Rigger did in her desire for love: "There is nothing bigger than God's love," etc. (See Chapter 3 for full handling.)

4. A sure way to take step five easily and surely is to think of the three basic urges and therefore the three basic fears as the three primary colors. For example:

Threats to the basic urge of life are thought of as red—the red blood of life.

Threats to the basic urge of love are thought of as blue—true blue love.

Threats to the basic urge of liberty are thought of as

yellow—or light, enlightenment. Light brings freedom.

When you learn to think quickly, "This is only a little old blue fear and I will quickly erase it," you will find your fears having to do with other human beings, your opinion of yourself, and of God and your relationship to Him will no longer give you trouble.

If you have trouble in getting the fear down to a color, or basic urge, ask yourself what it would take to make you blissfully and utterly happy. Then ask yourself what seems to be standing in the way or keeping you from that happiness. This will uncover the fear and you then can trace and erase it easily.

5. Continue to work with step three which, you remember, is to find new information, facts, truth that will set you free from fear by keeping your mind tuned in to the expanding ideas of others who are not afraid. Your daily paper is filled with proof that others are not afraid and are carrying out God's ideas for a better world as rapidly as existing conditions will permit them to do so.

For example:

Nuclear scientist Francis B. Porzel recently said that science "sees God on every frontier."

At any time we may find life on other planets. Let your mind dwell on this idea for a while. What would it mean to us earthlings if our scientists actually found intelligent, living beings much like ourselves on other planets? What would happen to some of our philosophical, theological and social attitudes?

One thing is certain, transportation is taking great

LIBERTY AND FREEDOM

strides forward. It is only about fifty years since the Wright brothers first flew an airplane. Hall L. Hibbard, Lockheed's genius who has been responsible for the design and development of many famous military and commercial aircraft, including the Lockheed Constellation, among other predictions made the following:

We will soon have family airsedans that will probably outnumber automobiles and will fly at 500 miles an hour and may even be run by "broadcast power," instead of today's fuels. New York and Amsterdam will soon be about ninety-eight minutes apart. Rocket ships will be used for long flights at speeds beyond our belief.

No one knows how much good is right at hand. Only God knows. If the ordinary person went at life and problems as the scientist does, to get answers and results, without the slightest trace of fear, how wonderful life on earth would be!

5

Overcoming Fears Concerning the Second Half of Life

Fear will make you old before your time . . . never stop growing and you'll never grow old . . . maturity without fear is a wonderful time to be alive . . . thoughts that will keep you feeling and acting young as long as you live.

STORY FROM LIFE:
The Woman Who Looked Back

> *I do not think seventy years is the time of a man or a woman,*
> *Nor that seventy millions of years is the time of a man or woman,*
> *Nor that years will ever stop the existence of me, or any one else.* WALT WHITMAN

The trouble with old age is that it has had too much adverse publicity. Hearing that old age is unpopular people get afraid of it, dye their hair and fudge about the number of their birthdays. Yet the second half of life can be filled with a beauty and happiness that youth can never know. One thing is certain: *fears about old age can make*

THE SECOND HALF OF LIFE

you old before your time.

For example, let me tell you about *the woman who looked back.*

This woman, whom we can call Mrs. Nolan, had been left a widow when her only child, a son, was three years old. She had worked as a clerk in a store to support him and herself and had given him a good education. After she had reached the age of fifty-five her employers began to find fault with her work and eventually discharged her. Mrs. Nolan became very much embittered. "It is the way they get rid of older people," she said. This had happened to other olding men and women at that store. Some of the employees had been there for many years.

Her son took care of her for a few years while she worked "now and then" but her son, who had been in love with a fine girl for several years, got married. Everyone was happy about Bill's marriage to Nancy except Bill's mother. Nancy's mother refused aid from the young couple. "I've had my chance in life," she said. "You've enough to do to establish a home and give me some grandchildren."

Bill and Nancy had helped Mrs. Nolan, who still lacked six years of being old enough to go on old-age relief (California state pension). She had expected them to continue helping her. But things had reached a crisis. Nancy was now expecting a baby and had to give up her job. Their before-marriage agreement was they were to have children and that Nancy would never go out to work again, once they had a child. Bill, having been brought up as an only child without a father "wanted to have several children."

These problems, threats to her future, so greatly worried Mrs. Nolan that she became melancholy, withdrawn and would hardly leave the house. Her son came to me on her behalf.

"Part of it is a bid for sympathy, to justify herself, to shame Nancy and her mother," Bill said unhappily. "But she's my mother and I love her and I want to do everything I can for her. Most of all, I want her to be well and happy. We gave her two of your books but she hasn't read them. However, she is willing to see you."

Mrs. Nolan lived in a small beach town. I arrived at her home about ten o'clock one heavenly morning. The sky was so blue, the sun so bright, the Pacific Ocean breeze so delightful that I had to argue with myself to park my car and go to her door instead of heading toward the beach. Bill had continued to keep up the yard, and recently had painted the little house for his mother. All this made such a good impression that I was doubly shocked when Mrs. Nolan came to the door. She wore a soiled bathrobe, with one pocket hanging by one seam, hem half out, dragging. Her uncombed hair had not been shampooed for several weeks and her pale face was a mass of self-pity.

"Come in" she said, in a tone that implied that one more trouble couldn't matter much. No smile. No warmth.

Having spent considerable time in prayer, thought and meditation on the case before going, and as always, sincerely praying, "Let the words of my mouth and the meditations of my heart be acceptable in thy sight, O Lord," I was not prepared for the words that did come out of my mouth. For I said:

"Self-pity will get you nowhere with me. Unless you are willing to cooperate and try to help yourself, I am not going to waste time with you. I can see only a limited number of people in person. In order to come down here today, I had to put aside the book I am working on. Your son is a fine young man. I felt certain that any woman who could do what you've done to bring him up would be worthy of all the help I could possibly give and more. I thought you were a going concern. Your son praised you highly. But I see you don't really want help. You only want pity."

Mrs. Nolan had stood silent while I scolded, her eyes downcast. Suddenly she began to weep. I felt like the lowest barnacle on the lowest bottom of the lowest ship.

"I do want help," she said presently. "I need help so badly I am scared." Then she told me what had happened that made her willing to see me.

Recently her son had brought her an apple pie in a beautiful plate. "Nancy baked it for you, mother," he had said happily and proudly. "Nancy is a wonderful cook. She bakes the best apple pie I ever ate. You'll say so too, when you taste it."

"That," said Mrs. Nolan, "was piling insult on injury. *I* used to bake the best pies in the world. Now, it is Nancy! Well, after Bill had gone I kept on thinking about everything and I was so mad I just picked up that pie, plate and all and slammed it down on the floor. Broke the plate, splashed pie all over the place. But I felt better. Got some of the anger out of me. But I felt ashamed too and afraid and realized I needed help."

It is my experience in working with people with problems that the one needing help has to want it and be very willing to ask for it. Otherwise, help poured on can become trespass and usurping of free will. No good can come from that. Mrs. Nolan convinced me she was serious about wanting to be helped. So we started to work.

Our first job was to get Mrs. Nolan to see that she was suffering from a three-phase fear, because all three of her basic desires for life, love and freedom were threatened.

No job, no financial help brought a whole flock of fears; not enough money, loss of prestige, damage to health, no money for doctors or food. This was also a threat to liberty. Bill had moved twenty miles away, and she no longer had a car. She felt things were closing in on her. Moreover, old age appeared to be a threat of helplessness, being unwanted, unloved and she feared she already had lost face with her son, status with the others.

Mrs. Nolan had been eating from the tree of death, that old, old *false belief that evil can overcome good.*

"Your basic problem," I said, "is that you have been trying to hold things still. You have been looking back at life and trying to hold everything just as it was at its highest best for you. Never can it be. Life forever marches on and we must move along with it or be run over, or shunted aside in the shallows of life where existence is dull, painful and ungainful. So stop looking back, my dear, start to look forward."

That, she was willing to try to do. Our next step was to look at her religious beliefs. We found she believed God did not love her. This belief had begun when her husband was ill and died so young. God had not helped him or her then. She never had trusted God since. Her anger at God and others was, of course, anger with herself for not being able to handle life. Anger ever is a defense against fear.

The healing of fear for Mrs. Nolan began with her new concept of God as all love, all wisdom and all power and an understanding of the spiritual laws which execute themselves. Her second step away from fear was to realize she did not have to try to break her fear habits, but instead to *walk away from them* by setting up new habits in the opposite direction. To do that she would have to *set a goal* for her life from there on. She would then have to use her creative power to think of what she did want, about how to fulfill her three basic desires for more of life, love and liberty instead of dwelling on what she did not want and feared would happen. She had to leave the past and walk toward a good future.

It took quite awhile to get Mrs. Nolan to see that she could attain such a goal. "But if you quit, give up, and drag along in life until you are of legal age to go on relief, you would only deepen your fears, resentments, shorten your life, damage your health and curtail your freedom,"

I told her. "Besides, the moment you received an old-age pension you'd lose status with yourself. It would mark you, in your own mind, as a less person. Nancy's mother is determined not to ask for help. You will hate and resent her all the more if you accept it."

Point by point Mrs. Nolan saw the truth that would eventually make her free from all her fears, and so, open a new life to her.

"All you can take with you when you go from earth is what you have become," I reminded her. "Don't just spend these autumn years of your earth life. Invest them in learning the spiritual laws, in learning how to use the power of your word, and overcome fear once and forever. You are too intelligent, too capable and too honest and you've been too good a worker just to sit down and quit and be entertained for the rest of your life. You would be sick of yourself."

Finally Mrs. Nolan said, "I already am sick of myself." She added, smiling, "You know what, I like you! You had the courage to scold me. Brought me to my senses." By that time it was noon and she wanted to offer me lunch but the kitchen sink was piled with dirty dishes and she wasn't sure there was any coffee in the house. Everything in the kitchen needed cleaning from floor to curtains to ceiling.

That first visit I asked Mrs. Nolan to start to walk toward her goal of becoming self-respecting as a means of overcoming her fears. Some of the changes she was to make at once were:

1. Polish all her shoes, put in new shoelaces to replace the knotted and broken ones.

2. Have her hair done.

3. Be out of her bathrobe and slippers before eight, mornings. For many years she had been at work by eight, away down in Los Angeles.

4. Repair, clean, wash her clothing.

5. Clean the house, curtains, and refrigerator; make all else as neat and attractive as possible.

"I don't see what all this has to do with my future," she objected, for her habits were deep.

"It is your present," I explained, "and out of it will grow your future. Your need is to order and control your future by what you do in the present. Your fears will drop in proportion as your self-respect and esteem go up. Emotions can take you forward or backward. Your surroundings greatly influence how you feel. Your need is to feel creative and happy with plans for immediate action."

"All right," she said in a spirit of cooperation. "I guess I'll get a new corset while I'm about it."

"Good," I approved. "And a new dress, too. You have to go through the motions of having self-respect and of being a going concern. A woman with a new corset and a new, becoming dress does not sit at home and mope. She puts them on and goes out to let people see how attractive she can be. Everyone enjoys seeing a well dressed, well groomed woman. Make some social plans too. Let it be a treat to people to meet you."

Was it just whistling in the dark? No! It was working

with the laws of life, love and liberty.

Mrs. Nolan was already on the way to overcoming her fears before I left that first day. For at the door she said to me, waving back at the house, "This will all be changed."

On my second visit I found it was changed—so clean, so sparkling that I went from room to room complimenting her on all she had done. When she put on her new corset and new blue dress I admired the good effect. People who entertain fears need a great deal of praise and admiration. I had gone to suggest her first step in financial independence for a flood of ideas had come to me for her. I had sifted them down to what seemed the best one. We went into it at once.

The idea was for Mrs. Nolan to work in the home of someone who needed her, where she would receive a salary, room and board and be able to rent out her own little house. This would make her independent of receiving financial help from her son. Earning would further still her fears and she would be with people and not alone, and could practice the art and science of love, which once perfected casts out all fear.

In setting up a goal for her financial independence, we began with the law, "Use what you have to get more of anything you want." And: start where you are. When I had asked Mrs. Nolan to write down a list of her assets she had said she had nothing but her little home which was free and clear of debt. The list I made up of her assets included: Time, which if put to work earns money.

Experience in selling. Experience in love. She could read and write, walk, talk, stand, see and hear. She could cook, keep house and drive a car. And while she showed me her new clothes I discovered another asset: she had a good sense of style and colors. In a corner of her bedroom was a thick stack of magazines about better homes and building. She had made some inexpensive, very pretty curtains for her bedroom.

Before I left that day Mrs. Nolan had agreed to run an ad in the paper and offer to take care of an older person and live in their home. My long-range objective was for her to save all the money possible, to start to buy a residence income lot toward the day when she could build income property and so achieve her final financial freedom. To help her concentrate on the good she desired and to take her mind completely away from things and conditions she feared, I had taken her a little gift. It was a small ivory statuette of the three famous monkeys who, in turn, see no evil, hear no evil, speak no evil.

"Nora Nolan," I said, "I want you to learn to be a good monkey," and we laughed about it gaily. It proved to be a good technique for her.

Her ad brought results. She accepted the job of looking after an eighty-five-year-old lady. "Helps me to remember my own blessings," said Mrs. Nolan. She liked the place from the first and they liked her. *Because she had a goal* she wanted to reach Mrs. Nolan "went all out," to give satisfaction to her employer. "Standing behind a sales counter trying to please the public for years helps me out now," she told me. Soon the daughter of the elderly lady bought a little used car for Mrs. Nolan's use. She started going to church again, making new friends and on her days off she went "realestating," looking at lots and income properties for ideas for her future project. She also had some time to read, study and attend an occasional lecture.

When a threat surfaced Mrs. Nolan commanded herself to "Be a good monkey, Nora." She was actively working at her determination to overcome anything that looked like evil with good.

By the time Mrs. Nolan's second grandchild had been born her affairs had progressed to the place where she was ready to build her income property. She had done no baby sitting. She had been too busy living a happy and constructive life of her own. They all visited and were friendly, but Mrs. Nolan never had idle time on her hands. When she was ready to start her project she had a relapse into fear. What if it didn't pay off? She was going to risk her all, to sell her home and finance her now clear income lot for the building.

"Of course it will pay off," I told her. "People will not stop having babies. People will not stop coming to southern California. People like you will continue to want to live in smaller quarters as they grow older. Build for them the kind of place you'd want for yourself. Make your apartments beautiful, colorful, functional for the kind of tenants you mean to attract."

Mrs. Nolan "had a session" with herself about her

fears, decided to go on "being a good monkey" and to proceed with her building project. I sent a business adviser to her, and recommended a good architect and contractor. Her project was declared to be sound and she went ahead.

Today Mrs. Nolan looks younger than her years. Nearly every one of her tenants as they come and go have in turn been helped by that energetic, and happy woman. She has a lot to say to them about spiritual laws, overcoming fear and never growing older and about "being a good monkey."

Mrs. Nolan often points out to her tenants that "being fired from that miserable little job that looked so big to me at the time was an act of God in disguise. I shudder," she tells them, "when I think how different my life would have been if I had stayed on that job." To me, she often said, "I shudder when I think what would have happened to me if I had not overcome all my bitterness."

Here are some ideas that will help the person looking forward to tomorrow:

1. *The person in love never feels old.*

The older we grow the more we need to give and to receive love. Keep your love light burning—stay in love.

2. *Make yourself necessary and welcome to others.*

Tell yourself: "God and my neighbor have need of me. And I am loved and secure and free." Then work at it.

3. *Never ask for pity.*

Pity is destructive and deepens fear. Seek to be worthy

of admiration. To be admired is to be encouraged.

4. *Don't worry about the future of the younger generation.*

Tomorrow's world will be better than it is today. We are ungrateful and uncooperative guests of God if we doubt tomorrow.

5. *Love will do more for you than money.*

Money alone cannot give you a sense of security and help in your old age. It takes love put to work to do that. If this were not true there would not be a hospital or any other charity organization in existence. I have known older people who had plenty of money but no love to give and so received no love and who fared badly at the hands of paid helpers. But love will see you through. The person who is sweet, cheerful, loving, grateful, interested in others will never lack for tender, loving care.

6. *Serenity keeps you young.*

Even old faces are beautiful if they are serene. For serenity expresses God. Serenity is a result of being free from all fear, and so from all tension, hate, resentments, feelings of injustice and inferiority. Get rid of hurry, worry, fuss and fret. These make you old. Serenity comes from good desires and desires fulfilled, and cannot come merely from quitting, from resignation. Serenity is constructive, happy. Being resigned is destructive because it is giving in to fear.

7. *Keep on loving life as well as people and yourself.*

A retired school teacher, greatly loved by all who knew

her and cared for tenderly in her old age, once wrote me, "I am still kicking and ticking," when she was ninety-five. Her letters were always filled with a zest for living with news of others and comments on the world and life.

8. *Develop new skills and meet new people.*

Dr. James A. Peterson, associate professor of sociology at the University of Southern California, said that the factor of age is only incidental to the problems encountered at retirement. He said it depended upon the individual's attitude and that everything can come to a seeming end, even at forty. He advises enlargement of human contacts and ways to be useful. I agree with Dr. Peterson. And, I would add, the TV chair and a desire to be merely entertained is deplorable because destructive. We are born doers. To sit down on the side lines of life is to increase fear and discontent. Be a doer.

9. *Never stop growing and you'll never grow old.*

Louis Kuplan of the International Association of Gerontology said that good health in an older person has a very definite relationship with learning. So never stop developing your mind.

10. *Be a good listener.*

The ministry of listening is fitted to old age. Everyone needs to be heard. Especially the young.

11. *Eat of the fruit of the tree of life and stay forever young.*

The fruit of the tree of life is high faith—three-phrase faith in God, neighbor and self. Always expect the best. If an unpleasant or threatening situation arises, use the power of your word to declare boldly "only good can come out of this!"

12. *Feed your spirit daily.*

Read your Bible. Read the Christian message in the New Testament. Read the great promises and meditate upon the truth in the Psalms. They will bring you peace and a renewed faith in God's love, wisdom, and power. Memorize the 23d Psalm and repeat it whenever you feel disturbed or alone, or fearful.

13. *Don't regret old age, call it good and enjoy it.*

Look at life as a total picture. Old age will then take its good and rightful place. In early life so much of our time, energy and attention must be given to the physical body. But it reaches a limit of growth and stops there. We need to take good care of our body because it is the house in which we live while on earth. It is our means of transportation and learning. We need to keep it holy for it is the "temple of the living God," and is God's channel for passing on the spark of life. But as we grow older the body does not need to be further built, only maintained in perfection. This leaves more of our time, thought and energy to develop our mind and spirit.

14. *The mind and spirit should improve with age.*

This is why the second half of life can be so satisfying, with a wonderful sense of growing, on-going, of freedom and new power. Of course, the best time to prepare for a happy, carefree, fear-free old age, is in our youth. For if we have learned the lessons of love early in life, we approach old age with only the one big job to do—to

THE SECOND HALF OF LIFE

learn more and more and more before we leave this earth plane to enter a new school for further Soul development.

Growing older? Well, what of it? Age and change are part of the process of life. *It is good. So fear no evil!*

We have seen steps six and seven in overcoming fear, at work in this chapter. Now, we must name them and look at them more closely.

Step six is: *When a fear arises face the worst that could happen.*

Step seven is: *After facing the worst that could happen, be willing for it to be so, for it to happen.*

This is what Mrs. Nolan did. There is much more to these two steps than could be included here. After we cover the next two steps in Chapters 6 and 7, we shall go back and go into these two fully. Because steps six and seven are actually a part of eight and nine as we shall see.

But now, we must get on to chapter six. I think it may well be the most important chapter in the whole book. It will certainly be the most difficult piece of writing I ever have done in my whole life. I planned to take it out of the manuscript again and again, only to feel that I must put it back. Every writer owes the best he knows to his readers. And this, regardless of any personal pain or cost.

6

Overcoming Fears of Death and the Beyond

Man's greatest desire is to live forever and keep his individual Self or identity . . . the serpent doubt, still is the most subtil beast of the field . . . eat of the fruit of the Tree of Life and live forever . . . death is not bigger than life . . . love is stronger than death.

STORY FROM LIFE:
The Man Who Was Afraid of His Shadow

> *Ye seek Jesus of Nazareth, which was crucified: he is risen; he is not here: behold the place where they laid him.* ST. LUKE 16:6

Death still is the greatest mystery in life. It still is the most formidable threat to man's desire for more of life, love and liberty. Death is one of God's processes in the circle of life. It is a good and necessary part of life. But without an understanding of these facts life on earth can be a miserable existence, filled with fears both conscious and unconscious.

For example, let me tell you about *the man who was*

afraid of his shadow.

This man, whom I like to think of as Thomas Worth, is one I never shall forget. He came to me one bright spring morning. Though I was expecting him, he arrived an hour early and I was still in the garden. I had just finished for the day and was setting a dripper hose under the Rangpur lime tree when I saw Mr. Worth coming up the driveway, heading for the front door. I called to him and he came back, catching me in sunbonnet, garden dress and muddy shoes. I remember I apologized for not shaking hands with him because I am an amateur barehanded gardener and my hands were a mess.

Mr. Worth was about sixty-five years old, tall, thin, conservatively and modestly dressed. He was slightly stooped, as if he had carried many burdens in his time. His step was slow, his voice low and tired. His dark eyes had the look of hurt and disappointment. But every ounce of the man bespoke his integrity. By letter and by phone Mr. Worth had told me his problem was illness. Though he had read several of my books he had not said he wanted to be healed. He had not asked whether I would pray with him. He simply wanted me to talk to him and maybe answer a few questions.

His first question was about the lime tree. New to California, he never had seen a Rangpur lime before. The fruit of this tree is a bright orange color when ripe, and varies in size from an English walnut to that of a normal-size orange. It is sour enough to cut your throat. At that moment the tree was in full bloom, covered by a blanket of white, heavily scented blossoms, the sweetest fragrance of all the citrus trees. It was alive with bees.

"I could smell these blossoms from the street," said Mr. Worth, who also loved gardening. "What do you do with the fruit?" he asked, as he picked a large one left from the previous crop and sniffed it with interest.

We sat down on the low brick retaining wall which keeps the earth of my garden in place (all Pasadena slopes south from the mountains) and I told him about the wonderful life in that wonderful tree—the most prolific tree on the place, bearing blossoms and fruits in various stages the year round. I told him I never could see it without thinking of eternal life and of the goodness of God and the abundance of mother nature. Then I told him about my experiences in using the fruit.

"I tried repeatedly to make marmalade of the limes using my orange marmalade recipe. But it always turned out too strong. So one day standing here and looking up at the thousands of golden globes I said, "Lord, please tell me what to do with this heavenly fruit you have created. Tell me what to do with it so that the marmalade will be as delicious as it is beautiful." And the Lord said to me, 'Peel half of the fruit you make up; the bitterness comes from the skins.' I tried it and it worked. I have varied the proportion of peeled fruits many times until now I have a recipe that is perfect. I call it tendertone, and make up about forty quarts of it a year. My husband likes it so well he has a small dish of it every day. It is crammed full of vitamins," I said.

"The Lord talked to you?" said Mr. Worth. He smiled a little, as an adult to a child, shook his head and we got up and went into the house. I took him to my office and handed him a copy of Dr. Gustaf Stromberg's book, *The Soul of the Universe* to read while I went to change. When I returned a little later the book was unopened. Mr. Worth was staring out the window, looking years older than his age, tired and hopeless. He brightened considerably as I came in and said:

"The Lord talked to you?" Then that little hesitant half laugh, that was all on the surface, with no depth. It came out rather lopsided, as if to say "I really shouldn't be laughing." I came to associate that strange little laugh with him as we worked together. "You talked to the Lord and he answered you," he repeated. "Well," he sighed, "if you can prove to me that there *is* a Lord—a God—anything beyond the grave . . ."

Thus our work together began.

This was his story:

When he was a child his father was killed in an accident leaving his mother with five young children of which he was the youngest, and very little money. His mother had "worked like a slave," to feed and care for them. About the time Thomas was ready for high school his mother died. "I always felt she worked her poor self to death for us, and then was cheated out of her just reward. She did not get to see how we turned out. We would have taken good care of her and made her old age happy.

But we were denied that privilege. My children never knew a grandparent. It is not fair."

When we got to his religious beliefs, Mr. Worth said:

"I never have been able to believe in God. I can't believe in a life after death and yet I want to."

We can understand the depth of Mr. Worth's fears for fear of death has many parts:

1. Fear of the unknown which is as old as man and once was useful to him in saving his life.

2. Fear of extinction of body, mind and spirit. This means total loss of identity as a living Self, a knowing self and a loving self and a free self.

3. Fear of having failed the purpose of life on earth.

4. Fear of never seeing or knowing our loved ones again.

5. Fear of punishment for possible wrongdoing.

Here doubt, the serpent, still is the "most subtil beast of the field" as described in Genesis, because doubt is a power and privilege given to man and is part of free will and therefore is good. We have the right to question, to doubt. But when we use this power of doubting to doubt the goodness of God, we have used it to harm ourselves. Eve doubted the goodness of God; she felt God had denied them something that was desirable to have. She disobeyed God's orders and promptly got into trouble.

Mr. Worth's suffering was a result of his doubting the goodness of God. He believed that evil, something he did not want, could overcome the desires of his heart.

FEARS OF DEATH AND THE BEYOND

Mr. Worth was a good, moral, honest man. He was not afraid to die. He was afraid that death ended everything. The dread of death, feeling cheated in life, always had been with him. The feeling was in the background when he was busy. But the thoughts came boldly forth and visited him in the stillness of the night. Lately, those thoughts came quite often in broad daylight. They came whenever he walked in the sun and saw his shadow. The shadow made him feel cold, unhappy, and fear clutched his heart.

I encouraged him to talk about how he felt when he saw his shadow.

"The sunset of my life is approaching," he said. "I feel that when my body dies that will be the end of me. This body," tapping his chest with a forefinger, "is boss. *It* is going to die. But *I* don't want to die, now or ever. That is why I am afraid when I see my shadow."

"Why, Mr. Worth," I said, *"you* couldn't die if you tried! Your life is the life of God. Death is not in your keeping. Neither is life. Life is in God's keeping. You, the individual Self, the Being God created, will last forever. When your body in which your Self or Life, now resides, becomes unfit as a dwelling place for your Self of Spirit, then it, or you will leave the unfit body. It is made of earth elements and will stay on earth. Dust must return to dust. But *you* will be more alive than ever before."

Mr. Worth sat motionless. He breathed deeply and said, "I am still listening."

I went on:

"The Bible understood is an authentic document of religious history. From Genesis to Revelations it tells us that man, like God, lives forever because the life in man is God. The great scholars tell us that the life, death on the cross and burial of Jesus Christ can be as well established as any other fact in ancient history. There is no doubt about it. The man Jesus Christ lived. He really was crucified, dead and buried but he *arose from the dead*."

"Is anybody sure?" Mr. Worth asked.

"Yes. It is a fact. The most important fact in all human history. There were plenty of authentic witnesses to this fact. There were the Jewish and the Roman authorities of the day, soldiers, apostles, and women who were early at the tomb. During the forty-day period which followed the resurrection, Jesus appeared at least ten times and in one instance to more than five hundred persons. These eyewitnesses could not have been the victims of mass hallucinations, an explanation which is sometimes given by unbelievers to account for what happened. There were too many witnesses and spread over a time period of forty days."

"People make mistakes," said Mr. Worth, groping for truth.

"Yes, but the truth itself bore witness to the resurrection. This is why the early church had such courage, both moral and physical and why it lived 'in spite of dungeon, fire and sword.' In spite of all that Rome did

FEARS OF DEATH AND THE BEYOND

to stop it. People then living knew people who had, with their own eyes, seen the risen Christ. A mere myth of such victory over death could not have kept the young church alive. It would not be alive today. And it is, and stronger than at any time in its history."

"But I am not a Jesus Christ," said Mr. Worth, sadly, almost in a whisper.

"You are at least as good as the thief on the cross," I reminded him. "And of the thief, Christ said, 'This day shalt thou be with me in paradise.' The thief did not have to do anything but desire, ask and believe. If you keep on desiring, and asking you will find your way through to a faith beyond a doubt."

"If I could just get this faith inside of my own mind or heart, as you have it," said Mr. Worth, "I'd be the happiest man in the world and ready to die. If I could find God," he said.

"You don't have to find God," I assured him. "God already has found you. There is no other way for a living soul to come into being except through God's life. The most human beings can do is to pass on the spark of life."

As we continued our work together, Mr. Worth coming several mornings a week, we went further into the real cause of his unbelief.

We found that he never had recovered from the shock of the loss of his father because the family had no established church or religion in their lives. "I think we believed in the power of our own work and the security of money," he said. "I have lived honorably, made a good living, met my obligations and never once asked God for help."

"Since the whole world had been created before you came on the scene and millions of years of improvement had been put into God's project, Man, you hardly had to ask God for help if you were alert to the opportunities around you. However, your whole life would have been different if you had felt gratitude enough to thank God for all the good you did have," I said.

"That is a new thought to me," Mr. Worth said slowly, thinking it through. "Maybe I have been too busy blaming instead of praising?" He had come to see that he long had been angry with God, and accepted the fact that anger and hatred are defenses against fear. His fear was that something could and would deny him the deepest desire of his heart—to live forever and to see his beloved mother again and to "learn that things do make sense."

My suggestion that he write down a list of his blessings, all those things for which he was truly grateful, proved to be the turning point in his studies about the meaning of life and death. But the lime-tree story continued to impress him more perhaps than all the other teaching. Of course I was daily in prayer for him that he might break through to the enlightenment he sought. But often he would say, "Tell me again about how the Lord talked to you." He would shake his head and laugh. "You are just a child," he once said. "You have the faith of a child's belief in Santa Claus. Do you also believe in

FEARS OF DEATH AND THE BEYOND

fairies?"

As the summer progressed we often walked out to see how the lime crop was coming along. Once when our shadows were sharp on the cement driveway he said, "You tell me not to be afraid of my shadow, that I need only to face the sun (I told him Light) and my shadow will fall behind. But it will still be there and I will still know it. You tell me to trust God, to believe all is good. Well, I am closer to doing that, but . . ."

But he still had fears and our studies continued.

I sometimes gave him a jar of the lime marmalade which he greatly enjoyed and always smiled and said, "The marmalade that the Lord made," followed by his strange little laugh.

I typed out long lists of what some of the greatest people on earth have said about their belief in eternal life, and some fifty passages from the Bible. Mr. Worth went over them carefully and on returning the material he would say, "Very interesting, but . . ."

But he had not yet found *his* answer. As our work continued Mr. Worth became well acquainted with my husband, Herbert James Mann, an architect and engineer. Mr. Worth's life work had to do with the housing industry and the two men found several interests in common. One night when Mr. Worth was having dinner with us my husband said something to him which helped him more than anything I had yet been able to do. He said:

"My wife's beliefs make sense to me because they satisfy my engineering mind. We know that nothing in the world of nature is lost. All energy for example, is forever conserved. We burn coal. It changes form to heat and light. But not one atom is lost in the changing. This is to me a most impressive fact about nature. Things change form but their inherent energy is forever conserved. This implies intelligence and a plan and purpose in nature. If mere energy, then why not mind and spirit? The most important thing about us must be our Soul, or individuality. It seems logical to me that Universal Life, which is intelligent, is wise enough to preserve its highest values, those of human experience. To think otherwise is to believe that nature fails at the very point where she doubtless is the most successful. It seems to me all the other is for the final, or big purpose. I cannot believe there is loss in nature or lack of a plan for man after earth life. Nature is wiser than that."

"Do you believe in heaven?" Mr. Worth asked anxiously.

"Not a static, finished heaven. The Church always has presumed to know all the answers. But I am convinced that life after death is far better, far more beautiful and *useful* than anything the Church presents. I think modern science is on the right track. Like my wife, I get help from Dr. Gustaf Stromberg's book, *The Soul of the Universe*. He looks at life with the detachment of a scientist. He seeks the true facts of nature."

"Nature," said Mr. Worth excitedly. "Nature!"

The tall candles had burned to their base before Mr. Worth went home that night, but in his heart was a

FEARS OF DEATH AND THE BEYOND

hope and under his arm my copy of Dr. Stromberg's book. I went to bed happy, sure Mr. Worth had turned the corner. The next time he came he brought notes made from Stromberg's book. Placing them on my desk he said, "Now I *know* the Lord really did talk to you. Now I understand the nature of it."

Stromberg's book is now out of print and has been for several years. I have permission to quote, here, some of the points in it which so greatly helped Mr. Worth; the same points my husband and I so often discussed:

1. Thoughts like sensations and feelings are attributes of Cosmos (God). For what else can they be? *A combination of atoms cannot of itself give rise to a human thought.* If we admit the cosmical nature of thoughts, we begin to realize the origin of ideas, which is the same as that of the ova genes which came to earth and determined the development of organic life as described in preceding chapters.

We have said that thoughts can be transmitted from one individual to another (telepathy) and there is then no logical reason why they cannot be transmitted from an individual to the Soul of the Universe and from the Soul of the Universe to an individual (inspiration). [Italics and parentheses are Stromberg's.]

2. We have given reasons for the belief that a Soul is indestructible, and that its most characteristic property is its capabilities of development.

3. We have seen how charity, tolerance and peacefulness are rewarded by longevity, happiness, and beauti-

ful mental development. Sometimes they are rewarded by death from cruel hands, but the profit to the individual is indestructible, since the development goes on for all eternity.

Since I have mentioned my husband's views in connection with Mr. Worth, I should add the following:

My husband, as an engineer, was tremendously impressed by the Appendix in the second edition of Stromberg's book. In it Stromberg sums up his faith, which was also published in *The American Weekly* of April 18, 1948. He says:

In the nonphysical world lies the fountainhead of life. . . . Nature apparently has foresight and intelligence, and it is capable of highly organized activity. Since an impersonal nature cannot have such characteristics, we are led to the idea of a personal God.

. . . and after death, when our mind is no longer blocked by inert matter, we can probably recall them all (our memories) even those of which we were never consciously aware during our organic life. Some of these memories will torment us, and others will bless us. Our conscience gives us an inkling of what we can expect in another world, where there are pleasure and beauty, as well as sorrow and pain.

This, it seems to me, is the Heaven and Hell indicated by the many new discoveries in modern science.

After reading Stromberg, Mr. Worth went on to serious study of scientist Du Nöuy's *Human Destiny*, and Mor-

FEARS OF DEATH AND THE BEYOND

rison's *Man Does Not Stand Alone*. We three had many long discussions together, becoming more and more agreed on the points we have endlessly repeated in this book: man's desires for more of life, love and liberty.

We said:

The more we learn of earth the more we expect of heaven and rightly so. In keeping with what we are learning and doing in this space age, with science telling us there surely must be "millions of worlds like ours, inhabited by some kind of intelligent beings" the old idea of heaven seems too tame and unfulfilling. Few scientists of today would be content to settle down in heaven and never try to go over to the next planet or invent a new travel machine, or perhaps try to make a trip back to earth again. "Nature," we said, agreeing with scholar-writer Thomas Troward, "could build a new body for us suitable to any environment in which we might find ourselves."

We talked about the need for expanding liberty. Since there can be no safety or growth in liberty outside of love our need is to express more of life and love and not less. Liberty therefore, should increase and not diminish after death. So our ideas of the greatness of God increase. God is the cause, nature the method by which God's work is carried out.

As our ideas of God increase so do our ideas of the importance of man, the individual and his potential increase. Therefore, death should open up to us more of life, more of love and more of knowledge that brings liberty than we have had on earth. I personally believe that this is a trick of nature—and she is full of such tricks—we desire ultimate perfection because it is our destiny if we continue to so choose. We are being offered something bigger, and better, more wonderful than our present ability to understand or appreciate.

As long as we said "nature," and not God, Mr. Worth went along with us. Thus he began to eat of the fruit of the tree of life—to build a consciousness of utter faith in God, which he called nature, to understand that the love of God surpasses our human understanding; to experience the fact that our love in return casts out all fear. Whereas once, Mr. Worth had felt "nothing in nature cares, everything is at the mercy of its natural enemies," he came to think: "Even what appears to be evil is good." He finally said to me, "You are right; the body is not the most important part of man. I can now laugh at my shadow. But my *shadow cannot laugh at me. I* am boss!"

This must be explained. In Genesis we are told that to eat of the fruit of the tree of life is to live forever. This point bothered Mr. Worth. We talked about it repeatedly. I told him this is what it means to me: We will live regardless. But if we *have no fear,* which is a *taste of death,* we are able to pass out of the body from life on earth to the next life without actually "seeing death." We are alive all the time and know that we are and know there is no death. We know what is taking place. There is such a growing literature on this subject

FEARS OF DEATH AND THE BEYOND

of witnessed instances of persons who made that kind of transition without losing consciousness that we need not labor the point here. Enough to say that Mr. Worth *came to believe he could do just that*. Hence his remark, "*I* am the boss."

The summer blazed and blossomed itself through the garden and our hearts and lives. I saw Mr. Worth less and less as he read and prayed and meditated more and more on his own account.

Fall came, hot and bright, filling the air with the fragrance of the ripening pineapple guavas, big as turkey eggs. Mr. Worth came in October to bring me a birthday present and to take home a bag of guavas which he so greatly enjoyed. "You are much happier," I said.

"Oh, yes," he replied. "I just wish I had learned all this before. Now I can say God and it sounds all right," he confided, followed by his little laugh.

Fall went away with the high winds and left some change of leaves and brought threats of winter. In December Mr. Worth came to bring me a Christmas present and to take home a large bag of ripe tangerines. He so enjoyed picking them one by one. His happiness had increased but his body seemed more tired than in October. Then winter threw itself upon the face of the earth bringing drenching rains. The rains gave way to winter sun like minted gold, coloring and sweetening the kumquats, which I generally preserve in March.

Mr. Worth came one day when it was very blustery, when it had been raining and there was sleet for a few minutes. He worried about the lime tree and so we went out to see it. There was a snowcap on Mt. Wilson. But there was warmth in Mr. Worth's eyes and heart, as we stood beneath the lime tree, now heavy with several lugs of enlarged fruit. (In California we do not say pecks or bushels for measure. A lug is a box holding about thirty pounds.)

"The tree is not harmed even by the sleet," said Mr. Worth, relieved. And we went back into the house and sat before the fire of oakwood. "I am looking forward to my trip," he said, just as he was leaving.

I almost muffed it. I almost said "Trip? Are you going somewhere?" But caught it in time. "Good," I said. "Remember, you will not travel alone."

He nodded and went away.

Then it was spring again over the earth and in my garden. Mount Wilson rose high and mighty and blue over to the north. One sunny morning I felt a terrible and sudden loneliness and left my office which is in the front of the house, to go down the driveway to the garden. The suffering continued as I paused beneath the lime tree. As I stood there in the warm sun a breeze ruffled the white blossoms, sending a shower of petals down to the brown damp earth. And then it came—that little half laugh of Thomas Worth.

Oh, it was as clearly his strange little laugh as ever I had heard it before. Then frightening silence. I began to pray for the man. A dreadful, heartbreaking feeling caught me up and burst through me in sobs and drove me into the house and into my prayer closet, into the presence of God in prayer. But I was not comforted. I walked in the garden again, still wordlessly asking questions of God. *Had it been my imagination? Could I be losing my mind?* There was no answer. Only a mocking bird on the rooftop singing a song of gratitude for life, love and liberty.

I went back to my office but was unable to work. About an hour later the phone rang bringing me the message that Mr. Worth had passed away about an hour before. He had wanted them to let me know. "He was happy and fully conscious to the very last," I was told.

A special message to the reader:

In all the foregoing I have tried to give the reader reasons why I believe we do not need to fear death or anything beyond this earth life. And now, if the reader can pardon my becoming personal, I should like to share with him the following:

This book was to have been finished in April 1961, and published in September of that year. The foregoing chapter was one that had been completed about as it now stands. In March of 1961, my precious husband, Herbert James Mann, was struck down by an automobile, driven by a young man in a hurry. He died five and a half weeks later of the injuries received.

The book manuscript had been put down and not picked up again until October of 1961. During the intervening time I often thought of the chapter on fears of death and felt I might change it because of the experiences I had during my husband's last weeks and have had since his passing. But after taking Chapter 6 out, only to put it back again several times, I decided to leave it, and to make the following additions:

Everything I felt and believed and discussed with Mr. Worth is now more firmly held than before the passing of my husband. Perhaps later, when I am able to work with it more objectively, I shall write about some of the experiences because I feel they belong to the world.

Loss of a loved one in death brings pain and shock beyond describing. At first there is a fear that we may never fully recover from that loss; that the soul scars may become part of our eternal Self. Always, we find it hard to let our good go from us. We instinctively hope to keep and enlarge our good. I believe that our loving Father God and our wise Mother Nature have given us this hope to prepare us for the reality that is to follow.

I am grateful for the love and prayers and letters from many friends including readers of my books whom I never have seen. Their love has picked me up, and carried me along as in a river at flood tide, sweeping me on from day to day and from task to task. In a very real sense their very thoughts and good desires for me have helped me to carry on with my responsibilities and so, to finish this book. Truly, *love is the healer*. Not time, as is so often misquoted. Love.

My husband was not only an architect and engineer but he wrote songs and had started life as an artist. He was getting ready to turn back to these first two loves of his life—music and painting, but he had to go home.

I am so sure that my husband is as much alive as I am, that I expect to meet him again and to recognize him. I even believe we will take up some of our conversation, so suddenly and for the rest of this earth life, interrupted. I feel certain that since God brought us together at one time for our mutual benefit, love and growth, He can do so again. I am further certain in my own mind that our desire, our deeply caring about, our free will choice forms the link that is never broken but that will draw us together again. We often discussed this point of life and we were agreed on it. Herbert always brought our happy and excited discussion on life after death to a close with these words:

"Oh, my dear, it is all so *much* better than we can ever dream of."

I am convinced that he was, and is, right about it.

Let us now go on with our lesson at hand. For I firmly believe that our learning on earth has an eternal value for us. And it always is later than we think.

7

Overcoming Fears of Tomorrow in Our Troubled World of Today

There is no place to hide from God and progressive good . . . The dream that makes men great also makes them fearless and free . . . there are no problems beyond man's solution . . . our fears are man-made . . . the evil in men cannot overcome the goodness of God.

REPORT FROM LIFE:
They Have a Dream in Their Heart

> *For God hath not given us the spirit of fear; but of power, and of love, and of a sound mind.*
> II TIMOTHY 1:7

Future historians surely will write of our day as the Age of Fear. The late John Foster Dulles once remarked that we are living "from brink to brink." A great many people seem to think we have nothing to look forward to but slavery or extermination.

For several years, while working on this book, I collected information on what kind of people in America are and are not afraid of tomorrow and exactly what they fear. After listing one hundred and fifty named fears I found they could all be classified under thirty-six headings—the fears of modern man. Further analysis proved these were all contained in the three basic fears we have talked about in this book; fear of loss of life, love and liberty. Or fear that the individual would be prevented from trying to fulfill his desires for more of life, perfect love and ever-expanding freedom of body, mind and spirit.

Happiness is the goal of every soul and is back of our hunger for perfection. Like God our Creator, we want everything to be good, very good. Threats of nonfulfillment of our good desires bring unhappiness and fear to some but not to others. Why? The longer I worked, the more a "why" began to appear.

My research uncovered a great many people in high places who do not fear tomorrow. But the viewers-with-alarm are more numerous, more vocal and seem to be gaining ground. Personally, I do not fear tomorrow. I greatly wanted to know how ordinary people like myself felt and whether the trend of "why" would run true with them as with the Big Names who make news.

Then quite unexpectedly I had the opportunity to make a personal survey which covered more than six thousand miles, six months' time and involved my questioning and listening to hundreds of people from many walks of life. The sudden loss of my husband in April had left me shocked with grief. But I was surrounded by the love and wisdom of my children, grandchildren, students and friends. Knowing me so well they decided work would be a stabilizer for me. At their insistence and with their loving plans and help, I set out early in May.

A full report of my findings would fill a book several times the size of this one. Here, I can give only a few highlights and some conclusions. To make these clear I must first tell you about where I went, how I worked, and the kind of people I questioned.

Where I went:

First, by jet plane, tourist class, to Hawaii, our fiftieth state which is made up of eight islands. After covering 2,550 miles in five hours' flying time, we landed in Honolulu. I was met by my friends Mr. and Mrs. Howard W. Wickersham and blanketed with leis, their warm welcome and enthusiasm for living. After newspaper photographs and a news story, the Wickershams, who have lived in Honolulu some fourteen years, lost no time in proving to me that there is much more to Honolulu than the hula. They drove me around the island to get my bearings, winding up at their lovely new home in Kailua, where I was to spend some time. It is complete with swimming pool, indoor garden with blooming orchids and, that afternoon, one bravely exploring lizard.

Howard is a supersalesman with City Mill. Eloise is secretary to Mr. H. W. B. White, Executive Vice President of the International Market Place Corporation. Their daughter, Joyce, attends the University of the Pacific at Stockton, California. These two energetic, happy, *fearless* and busy people were the hub of a wheel, with spokes of information and inspiration that reached out in every direction to the very rim of the wheel of island life and much knowledge of the Orient. I met many of their friends, including the famous writer, Anne Powlison, whom we visited in her home which is built in and around and on top of a rock—with a million-dollar ocean view. No fears there.

From the first I picked up the thread of the "why" I already had discovered. It was the Wickershams who "wrapped it up" for me—the essence of what my survey had uncovered and what we ought to do about it. But this point must come later.

Next, I went in an airplane not much larger than an overgrown bumblebee to Kalaupapa Peninsula on Molokai Island which was established in 1866 as Hawaii's leper colony. There I spent a few days in the home of Dr. and Mrs. Harry P. Kramer. Dr. Kramer was then in charge of the Hansen's Disease (Leper) Hospital, where he had been for nearly four years. (He has since left it to set up in private practice in Honolulu.) These two good Dutch people, made out of pure love, courage and ability were a great help to me. Even their dog, Whiskey, proved helpful. He was a living example of the fact that animal pets take on the disposition and some of the habits of their human owners. Every time Dr. Kramer kissed his lovely wife Meike, or made a remark of love to her, Whiskey, very old and somewhat feeble, lying with eyes closed, thumped his tail on the floor in happy approval. When Meike spoke to Whiskey, or petted him, he let her know he was grateful and filled with love.

During my travels I met many dogs. Every one of them reflected the courage or the fear of their owners. (Whiskey is the only dog name I recall.) I long have believed that where there is life there is love on some level and a desire to express it. If we would love as much as Christ Jesus did we would also learn how to cooperate with this love in all life, and so, to do the miracles he did by working directly with the power that controls the atoms and molecules.

The Kramers took me to see the rugged north coast of Molokai at Kalawao—the original site of Hawaii's leper colony. I absorbed the early history of the place as we visited the Church of Father Damien, the Catholic cemetery and the Siloama Protestant Church. I heard the story of the suffering, the courage, faith and hard work of the people who struggled with the dread disease of leprosy in those early days. And once again I was reminded that man was born to conquer, that there is a power within him that can overcome any threat outside of him. For today the leper (outcasts even before Bible times), or Hansen's disease, patients, get well and stay well. Even the idea of "unclean" and of a stigma is passing away. On Molokai I met many wonderful people through the Kramers and what time I was not talking I was listening. Some people were afraid of tomorrow; others, like the Kramers, were not.

Returning to Honolulu, I stayed at the Halekulani

FEARS OF TOMORROW

Hotel. There I talked to strangers, hotel guests, on the beach of Waikiki in the afternoon and in the surf at seven o'clock in the morning. I talked to the help, to people in shops, bookstores, drugstores, lunch counters, everywhere within my walking distance. Some were afraid; others were not. The "why" was holding true.

Friends came to Honolulu while I was there and so I met both the *Lurline* and the *Matsonia*. Going down long before boat time I talked to cab drivers, lei sellers, people old, young and middle aged; Oriental, Hawaiian and white Americans. Some lived there. Some were tourists. Some were stationed there and lonesome, homesick for the mainland. Some loved the island. Others hated it. Many were afraid. A few were not.

Several mornings I had breakfast under the spreading haw tree at the Halekulani with Dr. Gladys Falshaw, an authority on some of the questions of modern India. She had just returned from India where she had gone for additional information for the book she was writing, and for a personal interview with Nehru. Deeply religious, selfless and fearless, and having spent many years in India, she was a storehouse of facts and inspiration. Through her I met a great many other people, all well informed, all busy, all happy. None of them was afraid of tomorrow.

The leaders of the local group of Seicho-No-Ie, which is a Japanese Christian Truth movement under the guidance of Dr. Masaharu Taniguchi in Tokyo, invited me to speak to them one night and I accepted. These men and women were aged about twenty to forty. After my lecture they gave me their opinion on the very points of fearing tomorrow that I wanted to know. One young Japanese man gave me a quick run down on the theory of American freedom and why we will have to fight for it if we hope to hold it. He explained what he and others he knew were doing about it. I found no fear at the meeting. The "why" was there.

After the meeting Mr. and Mrs. Robert M. Nakata, a handsome young Japanese couple took me to a midnight Japanese supper where I ate (not too bravely) several varieties of raw fish and listened to further ideas of fearlessness and plans of tomorrow.

I also visited in the home of Mr. and Mrs. Gale Bakewell. He is a retired businessman who keeps up with the world. Elinor, his wife, is writing a book about Hawaiians along with her church work and many other activities. Former Pasadena residents, their views and interests are worldwide. Just home from a trip, they were planning another. From the *lanai* of their home where we sat talking, we looked out over their brightly blooming garden, rimmed with tall coconut trees, past the swimming pool, on out to the far garden wall whipped by ocean spray at high tide and beyond to the vast blue Pacific where we could see ocean liners heading for the harbor.

Some facts I had been reading in a book picked up at Bishop Museum came to mind: "Bordered on the west by the continents of Asia and Australia, and on the east by North and South America, the Pacific covers one third of the globe. Within its confines are thousands of islands."

"Is it all just a sitting duck?" I asked, thinking of those tiny eight dots on the map, entirely surrounded by water, and remembering Pearl Harbor in December 1941.

They did not answer me. They were too busy talking about their plans, their son Ted, his lovely bride, about the hopes of a good world, what they had learned on their trip. During the whole afternoon not a word of fear was spoken.

Tom Dickerson, formerly of Hollywood, a taxi driver in business for himself, was better than a guidebook. He not only answered every question I asked, from "What is the name of that tree?" to "Why is it you do not fear tomorrow?"—for obviously he had no fears of any kind. Another taxi driver who also told me he was from Hollywood said he cursed the day he had arrived on the island. He voiced sixteen of the thirty-six popular fears of today while driving me from the Halekulani to the Royal Hawaiian Hotel.

A very wealthy man whom I met at the Halekulani, retired, bored, doing nothing further with life, answered my question with: "The whole world is a sitting duck for Communist warfare." But he thought it didn't matter anyhow. Civilization already had gone to the dogs. Labor unions would yet ruin this paradise. He talked well and at length on all thirty-six fears.

Everyone said to be sure to talk to Dr. Alexander Spoehr and his charming and capable wife, Anne. "He has done a tremendous job in building up Bishop Museum until it is favorably known over the world," they said. "Anne is an artist and sculptress and has done outstanding work for the museum, too," they boasted. Fortunately, I did get to see them.

Dr. Spoehr is an anthropologist and museum director. The biographical data on this youngish man fill two newspaper columns. Yet from the moment I stepped into their home, high on a hill, and met their teen-age son and daughter, and was almost knocked down by the joyful welcoming of their dog—large as a colt and twice as strong, and filled with love—I felt at ease. The greatest people always are the easiest to get along with. They never have to pretend; never are uncertain of their position. They know what they have accomplished and what they are. "They're not afraid of anything," I thought. And all our talk before, during and after dinner proved this to be true. They were getting ready to welcome one thousand scientists who were coming to Honolulu for a convention, to talk shop, to exchange ideas. When all was sifted down it would be found that those ideas were all about how to create a better world for all men. For a true scientist is a man who "thinks God's thoughts after Him"—even if he starts out in believing in no God at all, as the Russian Communist scientists are said to do.

There were heartening, sparkling conversations, pictures of hopes of earth, assurances of the power of man to overcome any and all obstacles, and great respect for what early man had done. Talk of how man has overcome and will continue to overcome threats of nature. They were worldwide informed, with worldwide interests. Since my visit there, Dr. Spoehr has accepted the position of Chancellor Director of the East-West Center at the University of Hawaii.

People who understand the East-West problems see this new Center as a great step forward in people understanding people. Vice President Lyndon B. Johnson has said it could "play a direct role in breaking down the barriers that keep men apart and that promote international tensions." Fearless people get the big jobs done.

I visited churches, talked to members, ministers, teachers, tourists, beach bums, housewives, architects, building contractors, two bankers, and some very practical businessmen. Now, a woman can do a lot of talking and listening if she has nothing else to do in the amount of time I had at my disposal. On the jet plane, first class this time, going home, I felt I had used my time well.

Home, I sifted and classified my wealth of information, compared it with the answers to letters I had received from queries sent out before. These queries had gone all over the United States and mostly to people whom I never had seen, readers of my books. The trend of "why" was holding.

After resting a while I began the second part of my

travels, going frequently within easy driving distances of my home in Pasadena, over Southern California. I have space here for only two examples of what I found:

First, there was Budd Ross, in Los Angeles, who has traveled around the world for the past forty years, and was just home from a worldwide cruise. He said, "We are nearer world peace than we ever have been." He goes to Europe often—made five trips in one year. He said, "The intelligent Europeans do not expect war. The Russian Communist leaders are more afraid of the United States than we are of them."

Second, there was the family in Orange County who sold out, lock, stock and barrel to go live in the desert to avoid bombs and fall-out.

Finally, in September, I took the third part of my journey of questioning. By jet plane to San Francisco, where I stayed at the Sir Francis Drake and covered the Bay area. Later I went on to Chico, Sacramento and Nevada. Again the "why" some are, and others are not, afraid ran true. For example:

There was Peter James Wikel, certified public accountant, and his wife, Florence. They live in Larkspur. He drove me around San Francisco showing me improvements, talking of world conditions, including all the threats to humanity and the growth of his own business. After we had crossed Golden Gate Bridge he drew up at a vantage point where we looked back at San Francisco, bright in the afternoon sun. This fabulous city, on seven hills, whose buildings reach for the sky had a storybook look.

"One bomb in the Bay," said Mr. Wikel, "and all of it—" indicating the whole Bay area, Berkeley, Oakland, San Francisco, with a sweep of his hand—"boom—gone!"

"Leveled," I agreed. "Then what?"

Mr. Wikel smiled as only a man who lives his Christian religion could, and started the car.

In their home they showed me pictures of their travels, told me their plans for the future, and shared with me stories of people they knew who had overcome tremendous problems in life. They also knew some who were afraid. They talked of their daughter and her good husband and how the young couple built their home with their own hands. They drove me endless miles. No word of fear.

A hotel maid told me she "hated God." She expected we would all be blown up. She had no plans, no hope for tomorrow.

Another maid in the same hotel told me happily of life in America, her deep gratitude for the privilege of being here and what life had been like under Hitler and of her abiding faith in God. She was filled with plans for tomorrow.

By private car I went to Chico where I talked with ranchers and others. I heard a lot about rotting food, surpluses, labor union problems, water problems, marketing conditions, extravagant government spending and horrible mistakes, but nothing of fear. By Greyhound bus I went from Chico to Reno. The long trip gave me hours of talking and listening. For example:

A man in a soiled suit and his wife in a rumpled dress told me they were going up to Reno "to do a little gambling." Nothing mattered anyhow. Humanity was lost. And gambling was fun. Especially when they won. They were living on California old-age pensions (charity). He told me about his new glasses "for free," and she told me about all the new dental work she had just had done which "cost her nothing." They had many fears and they felt it was wrong of the government to send money to foreign countries when the "old people of America need it more."

In Reno I was a guest in the pleasant home of Mr. and Mrs. H. H. Atkins, the first time I ever had seen either of them, but they were not strangers to my heart. Of grandparent age, each had been alone for some years, and were newlyweds of a few weeks and radiantly happy. They were anxious for me to know there is more to Reno than gambling. They talked about their church, his work, their lives, books, past history, God, present world conditions, threats of man against man. He is an attorney and part of the colorful past history of Tonopah, Nevada. Information flowed from their minds as freely as the bubbling water in Truckee River that flows through the town. Mrs. Atkins drove me around to see the beauty, worth, creative and constructive part of Reno, introduced me to friends, the minister of their church, and brought others into conversation. They knew fears all around them. They had none of their own.

FEARS OF TOMORROW

Then my friend Mrs. Emory M. Marshall came to take me to her ranch home near Minden and Genoa. We took turns talking and listening, pausing only when her car, with a built-in-conscience squawked unpleasantly when she pushed it past eighty-five miles an hour, which was easy to do on those great broad highways. Mrs. Marshall—Helen—was born in Santa Fe, New Mexico. Her husband was a mining engineer. They had lived in many places and had traveled widely. She was just home from Europe where she had gone to see her son Mike and his family in England before he took off for Nigeria where he is adviser to the Nigerian government. By the time we came to historic Carson City, we had warmed up in our talking.

We sat in her comfortable, beautiful home, a great two-story brick, a hundred years old, painted white, tiled and carpeted and modernized inside, and talked about yesterday, today and tomorrow. Her dog, having accepted me, took me on long walks on the afternoons when she was busy and showed me the spots nearby where the Mormons had made history years ago, and where the Candy Dance is held Saturday nights.

On free afternoons we sat in the vast enclosed shed, covered porch, that faced east and looked out across the empty spaces of Nevada countryside. It was soul developing, mind-stretching and spirit healing for me. At about three in the afternoon the mountains behind the Marshall home started to cast a shadow that flowed, a creeping carpet of changing colors past their acres, down and down the gently sloping fields toward the highway miles beyond. After a while the shadows completely covered the great valley and the little towns and ran up the slopes of the mountains on the far eastern side of it.

Helen and I talked about going through the Valley of the Shadow of Death. We had much in common, for each of us had lost her husband since our last meeting. We found we feared no evil, however deep the shadows of the afternoon, however long the night, however threatening the problems of the world. Helen talked of Europe, people, music, trends, books, which she has by the hundreds—several written by her sister Ruth—her church, her children—Mike, Pete, John, and Bonnie, all in different parts of the country and the world, all working at great problems. About her grandchildren—their future and the great-grandchildren. She was getting ready for a one-woman show of her paintings and thinking of going back to Berkeley to live. She showed me some thirty of her paintings which sang with the desert colors and pleased the eye with form. They reminded me of God, peace and eternal life. No daubs of confusion. Helen had managed to get her own strength, courage, faith, love and a sound mind into her paintings. They helped further to heal my grief. Perhaps beauty and harmony, growing out of love, always heal.

Helen took me to visit friends at Lake Tahoe. Another day, to meet her son Pete and family who run the "big ranch." Watching their Basque sheepherder tromp newly shorn wool into a woolsack (so expertly that he gets four hundred pounds into the sack), with the blue sky and bright, hot sun overhead, and peace like a benediction over all the Nevada land, it was difficult to imagine that the American people ever could be afraid of *anything*. But they are, as my records continued to prove.

Taking a Greyhound bus from Carson City back through Reno and down to Sacramento, some talked about their fears. Not all. One seat companion, a young widow, with a daughter just through school and starting out in the business world told me of her great good fortune just at hand. She was overflowing with joy, gratitude, love of her daughter and of life, liberty and her "little office job" that had seen her through and let her give her daughter a good education. She laughed at American fears. She hadn't a one.

In Sacramento Teresa Hihn Moore, a dynamo of energy, a guidebook of reliable information and an expert driver of her Mercedes-Benz took me around, even to Folsom. But we did not visit the prison. We looked at valuable real estate. We visited a friend of hers, now almost eighty-five years young who was busy writing a book which I believe will startle the whole thinking world when it is published. We heard about her plans for an own-your-own apartment for retired people to be built on her twenty-five acres. We looked at her unusual button collection and met her daughter who is a successful playwright and her son-in-law who travels for the state of California. They were just home from a trip to Alaska. Dozens of interesting, crackling, creative ideas, peoples, and plans came up for discussion. They knew many people who are afraid of tomorrow but they were not.

Staying at the Senator Hotel, I took time to talk to strangers and employees. Some were afraid; others were not. I walked in the Capitol grounds and talked to more people, attended church and heard a fearless sermon by the Reverend John Hinkle, minister of Christ Unity Church whose congregation is so large no church holds it. They meet in a theater. I talked to Michael Arnold, minister of the Church of Religious Science there, and author of *Blessed Among Women* and other inspiring books. I met many members of their church and heard about their plans for a new building. But no word of fear.

By train from Sacramento to Oakland and from there by bus across the Bay Bridge back to San Francisco, I had more opportunity to talk. On the train, which had started from Chicago, there were a young couple with five red-headed children, the youngest an infant in arms. They had pulled up stakes and left everything for greater freedom—more life, out West. Their problems and their courage put my heart on its knees in admiration. Pity them I could not. They had no fear. But in the same car was a well-dressed, middle-aged couple obviously unconcerned about money, so fearful of tomorrow that their faces were drawn, their eyes filled with discouragement and unhappiness. Well educated, they talked of the world's problems and thought the United States was doomed.

Coming home from San Francisco by train I continued to talk and listen. Some had fears. Others had none.

What does all this vast amount of information, the thoughts, feelings, faiths and fears of these hundreds of people, which adds up to thousands when we include the people known intimately and talked about freely by the people to whom I talked? What does it add up to? *Hope of Earth!* A way out of fears of tomorrow! Let me tell you.

People without fear of tomorrow all have one thing in common, regardless of how widely they may differ in all else. This: they all have a dream in their heart which *they expect to make come true.* And this, without a single exception. The greater number of them were well informed on current events, past history and trends for tomorrow. Having a real stake in the future kept them informed of the day. They saw life as unlimited.

People with fear may be divided into many classifications according to their specific fear and how many different fears they entertain. But they all had one thing in common, without a single exception. *They had no big personal plan,* no *dream in their heart* even though they were working to earn a living, and many of them were fighting for freedom on one or more fronts. Many were life-long church members. A minister's wife was one of the most fearful of all. The quality that characterized the most fearful was that they looked backward. "Things will never be as good as they once were," they moaned. The fearful limited God, themselves and their fellow men in their views of tomorrow, even those in high places.

Now, we must take a closer look at the fearless ones if we are to benefit by the survey and overcome our fears of tomorrow. We should first look at the dream in their heart.

The dream in their heart:

1. The big plans of the people who do not fear tomorrow were as varied as the people themselves. But their dream is essentially the same. All of them are dreaming of something bigger, something better, something more than they now have, or are, or know or can do. It is the dream of expansion, growth, but always it is to bring more freedom of body, mind and spirit when it comes true. Their dreams are not just for themselves alone; they include a better world for all men.

2. *The more their dream means to them the more sure they are of the future.*

Theirs is the dream that makes men great, fearless and free. It is the dream that never dies. It never is completely fulfilled for no sooner has part of it come true than the dreamer sees farther ahead, feels new desires for more and more. They are constantly seeing new possibilities for themselves and the whole human race. Something leads them on and on.

3. *This group is in the minority, and greatly so.*

People with a dream in their heart keep their consciousness on such a high level of faith that all their acts and thoughts and plans are creative of good. They simply do not tune in to failure, defeat or fear ideas. I think of them as the "remnant" of earth who always exist in every age and who pick up the pieces and rebuild the world after the other class has destroyed things.

4. *Theirs is the Dream of God.*

Their question is, not how soon will nuclear warfare begin or at all, but rather: Can we trust God to see us through the threat and probability or actuality of such a war? These people with God's Dream of expansion and growth say, "Yes, and all the way."

Yes, the findings would fill several books but we must hasten on to a few conclusions.

1. *There is no place to hide from God and progressive good.*

More people, money, ideas and love are working for the fulfillment of men's good desires than ever before in human history. We are not going from brink to brink of despair and ruin, but from *peak to peak of achievement*. The trouble is, we are moving so rapidly we hardly have time to cover the lowlands between the peaks. This creates confusion which opens many to fear. All the frightening and knotted problems of today are man-made and can be solved.

2. *Humanity is not going to the dogs.*

It is going to God. For to find God, the final part of the Who, What, Where, When, How and Why of the story of man is man's greatest desire. Science, religion and philosophy are headed in that direction. They always have been. But now, each recognizes the claim of the other and all are working together. A few evil men with blood on their hands and fear in their hearts and therefore lies and violence, cannot stop tomorrow's good. Evil breaks the law of love and is therefore stupid and doomed to eventual failure. Good is from God and good men will bring it into reality. There is nothing bigger than a good man except God.

3. *Nature will never run dry of creative ideas.*

Civilization will not break down, wear out or blow up. The human race seems to go down for a while, but never out. During the time immediately after Napoleon had wasted Europe with war, many wealthy and titled men committed suicide because the end of things had come for humanity. But right then steam came in and a whole new world of wealth, wisdom and happiness followed.

4. *Peace for profit and progress.*

This is the electronic and space age. What will we not do? And find? And learn? If we can keep the peace we will discover we do not need a war economy which so many fear will break America. We may well have come to the end of the threat of war because there now is no alternative to peace but death. All the leaders in the world know this. People do their greatest growing in years of peace. We are coming to it, peace for profit.

5. *Money is not security.*

The popularity of what I call the Communist "belly security" is fast losing ground. Millions already are learning the fallacy of money being security. "Security is never enough. To all of us must come the knowledge sooner or later that the only true security is of God," said Arthur J. Morris, banker and founder of the Morris Plan. The many are starting to talk about what the few always have known: security comes from knowledge, ethics, morals, character, love at work in individuals. Millions are now agreed that men, arms, firepower, laws of the land, cannot save even our lives, let alone protecting us from fear. Some are learning cooperation. But are there enough? And in time? Yes. For example:

Einstein said that if two per cent of the people on earth would decide on what they wanted to do with the world they could control it. People with God's dream in their heart do not want to control the world. They want conditions set up so that every man can carry a dream in his heart and be left reasonably free to try to make it come true. They see that in this method lie the safety and growth of the human race. That necessary two per cent already exist and are learning of each other. They will not stop their fight for freedom until it is won.

6. *The American people still believe in their own power.*

They still have the spirit and mind that gets things done. They still believe in the integrity, goodness, power and common sense of their fellow Americans and other peoples of the world. If for no other reason I feel my survey was worth all I put into it to learn this much about our America. People with God's dream in their heart prove the truth of Paul's statement which heads this chapter. He says:

"For God hath not given us the spirit of fear; but of power, and of love, and of a sound mind." It comes in a letter from Paul to the young Timothy, to encourage him. The truth it contains is just as alive and reliable today as it was the day Paul wrote it some nineteen hundred years ago.

Paul's words imply that the spirit of power, of love and of a sound mind are directly opposed to fear. In life that is exactly what we do find as every psychiatrist, psychologist and religious counselor can testify. That is what I found: the spirit (intent, purpose, nature) of love, power and a strong mind is absolutely and irrevocably opposed to fear. It is psychologically impossible to think of God as all power, all wisdom and all love and to continue to fear. *This is the dividing line between fear and faith in tomorrow. It is the "why" the survey uncovered.* As one doctor put it, "Anybody who is afraid of tomorrow is just plain nuts."

7. *Tomorrow's world will be free.*

The fight for freedom will go on. No man, no race, no country, no church, no political organization can for long keep other men imprisoned if they want to be free. This is the age of revolution which will eventually be proved to be good. All men instinctively know they were born to be free. There is something inside human beings that is bigger than prison bars, armies, guns and unjust laws of the land. "There are more men ennobled by study than by nature," said Cicero. And today millions realize there must be liberty in which to study and learn. We work against nature at our own peril. And nature says, "Grow, forever."

8. *Public freedom is assured.*

There are two sides to freedom. We must look at both of them. The freedom of the individual as given in the American Constitution and Bill of Rights will come for millions and sooner than many may now think. This public freedom of press, speech, peaceful assembly and religion, once experienced, is dearer to man than life itself. These conditions are necessary before man can work through to the higher or private, individual freedom.

9. *The higher freedom will come slowly.*

This is the point that was so clearly seen and "wrapped up" for me by Howard and Eloise Wickersham in Honolulu, briefly noted before. We sat talking for hours after dinner one night, aware of, but not unduly listening to, the glorious tropical storm that was whipping and pouring down outside their home. We were listening, I think, to our own souls' promptings. Together the Wickershams got it into words about like these:

"The public freedom will come, but happiness or good will not necessarily follow. Look at what millions of Americans do with it now. Unless we go on to that higher freedom what hope is there for the individual at the mercy of the mass?" This higher freedom they—Truth students for years—said "must be what the teachings of Jesus explained. Each man must learn to use his powers in such a way that no other man ever can take advantage of him again. Nor harm him. Each individual must become as self-sufficient as was Jesus Christ. Each man should be able to overcome sickness, poverty, worry of all kinds. There should be more to life than just working to earn a living. There should be a joyous use of the power to create."

Exactly! And it comes now only to the few who learn how to *stir up the gift of God within them*. This gift of God is the power within us which we are to use to make our dreams come true. In doing so, many are now learning to use the power inside themselves to create and to control conditions in their individual world outside. This truly is the higher freedom and is the final great aim of man on earth. This the Bible clearly teaches from Genesis to Revelation. We can expect a tremendous change in the Christian world as more and more leaders begin to see this truth about life. When we start to learn how to use the power God gave us we put aside fear forever.

10. *My final conclusion:*

We have too many "groan" people and not enough "growing" people.

How can we overcome fears of tomorrow in our troubled world of today? We can *learn to trust God all the way*. To do so is to take step eight in overcoming fear.

"Well, yes," someone may say, "it is true that God cannot be mocked. But He can be refused. We do have free will. What about all those people who use their freedom for destructive ends? If it will take a long time for individuals to grow into the higher freedom, what is to become of us meantime? The very weight of numbers of those other people . . ."

Let us go on to our next chapter and take step nine to overcome fear. For this, we shall find, is the most important one of them all.

8

There Are No Fears Beyond Your Control

Master plan for overcoming all fears . . . your future is in your hands . . . thought habits can make or break you . . . the most important thing to remember.

STORY FROM LIFE:
The Man Who Lived with Monsters

> *With God nothing shall be impossible.*
> ST. LUKE 1:37

A few years ago a young man just out of the Army and home from his stint in Germany came to see me at the request of his mother.

"He is so discouraged, has such a gloomy outlook on life," she said, "that his father and I fear he will get sick or lose his mind." She wanted me to pray for him and, "if possible to cheer him up, and get a better viewpoint on life." He once had belonged to the church, but he had lost interest and no longer attended.

I like to think of that young man as George West. George, because he, too, had a dragon to slay; West, because he had a heart and mind that belongs to the Western world of our day. He talked easily and to the point. But his face and voice were expressionless; his attitude was one of calm, hopeless resignation.

"I came," he explained, "to please mother. It's little enough to do for her. But I don't expect you or anyone else to help me. Mother lives in a world of unreality. She goes to church, joins her friends in doing good works to save the world. This keeps her happy, for which I am grateful. But they are not going to save the world. Nothing can save it."

"What makes you so sure that nothing can save the world? And to what is it to be lost?" I asked.

"Statistics are against us," he replied. "There aren't enough people worth saving or who even want to be saved. It is one vast Sodom and Gomorrah. Once, men became so evil that they brought on the flood as a cleansing measure. Next time, it will be fire and the quicker the better. Human beings have become monsters. I know. I had to live with them for years and now I read about them and see them everywhere." He then reeled off statistics about the "wickedness and stupidity" of our day. "Look at the picture in the United States today, wealthiest country in the world. Right now two thirds of the world still go hungry. But as soon as other nations get education and money they do the same destructive things. These spell doom for humanity," he said with an air of conviction.

"You may be absolutely right," I said, which surprised

him. "If everything does end that way, I wonder how God will feel about His Project, Man? It surely would be heartbreaking when you consider the millions of years and the billions of human beings that have gone into His noble experiment."

George sat glooming but made no comment so I picked it up again:

"Do you suppose that if among all the worthless trash of humanity—the monsters you've described—God found *just one* person alive in the world today who measured up to His expectation that God would then not feel so badly about His experiment? I mean, if God found even *one* created being a success, wouldn't it prove to God that His idea had been sound; the pattern perfect? Do you suppose it would encourage God to try another few millions of years and throw another few billions of beings into the test tube? And do you personally think it would be worth the trying?"

"Well," said George thoughtfully, "if *one* turned out perfect it would prove the idea was sound. But even God can't go on wasting millions of years and billions of people in an effort to create a perfect man."

"What better has God got to do with His time?" I asked. "Should He go back to creating prehistoric creatures, more suns and blazing stars? Or is His creature man, with all his faults, His highest and best and most satisfying effort so far?"

"God could better put His time to creating something more worth while than man who has let Him down," said

George. "There must be a creature higher than man."

"Could be," I agreed. "Scientists are now telling us that there are billions of planets and suns like ours and that doubtless some of them have intelligent beings on them. But as yet, we earth people have not proved that they exist. So perhaps Project Earth Man is important to God. In what way do you think God failed in setting up His plan? Was it because He gave man free will which he uses to get himself into trouble? Would the Project have worked out better if God had made man a puppet, pulled by strings?"

At the question of free-will man vs. puppet pulled by strings, George exploded. He talked for three solid hours, almost without pause. I served as the sandpaper against which he struck his matches of ideas, one after the other. When they flared up he saw a new light, and saw it for himself, which he used to examine his own beliefs and fears. He took up events of history, time and the march of man, the futility of acts outside the law of love and what he felt was wrong with the half-practice of the Christian religion. He ended up with, "Hell, it's never been tried!"

When he had about talked himself out I felt he was ready for the question I had been holding back. I put it to him: "What is there," I asked, "to keep *you* from being that one person God can count on?"

After a great deal more talk on his part, while I again ministered by listening, George finally said, "Nothing. Nothing but myself, I guess. My own mistakes; my own free-will acts. Perhaps I'm a monster, too—of a different breed, maybe, but a monster."

It was some time before George realized that in his statement he had solved the problem which he had thought was beyond solution. After talking about it at length we were ready to examine his fears and what had given rise to them.

"You are afraid that God's millions of years of work will be wasted; that the experiment, man, will fail through a fault of man himself, and that humankind will be annihilated," I said. "And further, that it ought to be so annihilated."

"Exactly," George admitted, greatly relieved.

We looked up the word annihilate. Webster says it means "To reduce to nothing; as to be utterly annihilated. To destroy the form or essential character of, so that the thing as such no longer exists. To destroy the force of; to make void."

We studied the meaning of the word annihilate at length.

"But how could God annihilate the force in man?" I asked. "The life force in man *is* God. As Jesus taught, God is within you. Can God annihilate Himself even to the degree that He is invested in man?"

"Well, no," said George, reaching out for firm ground for his groping desires for answers that would comfort and sustain.

"Then man cannot annihilate himself either. To do so would be to annihilate a part of God. Can man—the created—go above God his Creator?" I asked.

George worked the idea up and down and around. In a burst of enthusiasm he said, "I guess man just has to continue to exist no matter how damned foolish he may be."

"I think so," I agreed.

After a long silence George said, "Looks like God is stuck with us. Having given us free will there is no way to get rid of us. And what's more, we are stuck with ourselves, too."

I nodded in agreement.

Much later George added: "It may be that we, God and man, are bound together for eternity. There probably is no way of separation."

So began our studies together. George left my home that day with a goal in life; with a tremendous dream in his heart, perhaps the most important dream a man ever can have. For he had made a holy promise to God, himself, and without his recognizing the fact at the time, a promise to humanity. It was this:

"From here on God can count on me."

Looking a bit farther at George's fears will help us to overcome all fear. His fear was this: God will be defeated because man will fail. Man will fail because he does not sufficiently care to try to discipline himself thoroughly for success.

In George's mind, that evil power, that something greater than God was man's baser, animal nature, his spiritual immaturity, weakness and ignorance. The very fact that George was so concerned that he wanted God to succeed was a kind of proof that God's plan would not fail. George began to heal from the moment he saw that truth. Always it is the truth that sets us free from fear.

He went from that point to researching the story of man on earth; to watch in awe the steady growth through the ages of this being God created. He convinced himself that man often is down but never out, that he can right himself after every mistake, every deluge. As George raised the level of his own consciousness because of the new determination in his heart, he left the old level of fear and went up higher. There he soon drew to himself facts, truth, new friends who were not monsters but fearless, happy and busy people. He began to feel and to say, "There are no fears beyond man's control."

George wanted some facts to share with others. Here are some that helped him:

1. *Until a man can be led by the spirit of love he is driven by fears.*

Primitive man thought "These things are bigger than I am" and so was afraid. Dangers around him forced him to think. His desires—and threats to their fulfillment—led him to try, inquire, acquire, experiment, dare and so, to grow. It was not the mind nor the body strength that kept man marching onward and upward. Many modern scientists today agree with religionists on this point. Lecomte du Noüy in his monumental book, *Human Destiny* makes this clear. Man's free will to choose—for moral, spiritual growth—is the power that led him forward and this same power wrongly used holds him back. We still face the choice: love or perish. Ever it is his spirit, feeling, intent, purpose, deep desire which have directed man's mind and body and brought him from earliest beginnings to now.

2. *Perfection is possible.*

The following (from Du Noüy's book just mentioned) helped George greatly:

> Human progress, therefore, no longer depends solely on God but on the effort made by each man individually. By giving man liberty and conscience God abdicated a part of his omnipotence in favor of his creature, and this represents the spark of God in man . . . Liberty is real, for God Himself refused to trammel it. It is necessary, for without it man cannot progress, cannot evolve.
>
> The animal struggle against nature, against the elements, and against the enemy, the "struggle for Life," from which the human form finally emerged after ten million centuries, is transformed into a struggle of Man against the *remains* of the animal within him. But, from now on, because of his conscience, it is the individual alone who counts and no longer the species. He will prove that he is the forerunner of the future race, the ancestor of the spiritually perfect man, of which Christ was, in a sense, the premature example, by emerging victorious from the fight. Thus Christ can be assimilated to one of the intermediary, transitional forms, perhaps a million years in advance of evolution, Who came amongst us to keep us from despair. He in truth died for us, for had He not been crucified, we would not have been

convinced.

Consequently, any restriction to liberty of conscience is contrary to the great law of evolution, that is, to the divine Will, and represents Evil.

George finally said, "So we have to let them be monsters if they still want to be, since God Himself does not force them to grow."

3. *Fear always springs from ignorance.*

It long has been known that the fears and phobias of primitive peoples are far more numerous and more intense than those of highly civilized people. Psychologist Marie Hackel Means directed a project at Alabama College testing and tabulating the fears of one thousand students. It was determined that the higher the IQ the less the student was subject to fear. Fear belongs to cave days. Caution is good and necessary. It belongs to the space age. Caution is seeing a danger and avoiding it. Fear is the feeling of being at the mercy of something outside of oneself.

4. *Look forward to something better in your own life.*

Every experience in life, all events of history should teach us plainly that we are being prepared for a higher form of life or beingness. Every new discovery of science opens the doors to vast new areas of facts that exist but have not yet been touched. It is a chain reaction. Expanding knowledge creates new desires to know. Man is being taken upward and forward as rapidly as his willing cooperation will permit. The individual's progress is not held back to the level of the group. For growth is a matter of morals and fearlessness. It is an individual matter.

5. *Look for constant improvement of the human race.*

All people desire to be better. We carry around a blueprint of perfection in our heart, as great men of all ages have told us. Plato says that perfection exists, for if it did not, we could not think of it. He and other philosophers and religionists say that the seed of perfection is in God; that our desire for good and for perfection is God seeking to awaken our consciousness and draw us to Him. This is why prayer works, and why we want to pray.

6. *Respect your longings and yearnings.*

Our longings for good for ourselves and others are the voice of God inviting us to come up higher. All the roads of yearning lead home. Home is first cause, God, where our desires come from, and where fulfillment is to be found. Good moves in a circle.

7. *Your future is in your hands.*

"As a man thinketh in his heart, so is he," says the Bible. If we will control our thinking we can control our future and eliminate fear from our lives.

In Chapter 7 we learned that the people with the dream that makes men great and fearless and free had taken step eight to overcome fear which is: *Trust God to take you through.* Knowing that you can count on God is faith of the highest order.

In this chapter we saw how George West took step nine in overcoming fear by being the kind of person God can count on. This is a three-level love of God, neighbor and self, which casts out fear. It is love in action. We cannot long hold that dream in our heart, without changing for the better. We cannot entertain the idea that God can count on us, and not begin to realize we can count on God. We come to know beyond doubt there is meaning to life, with help and protection to be had for the asking and accepting. When we come to that we are safe and secure forever.

"But I am not perfect," someone may say. "I cannot take that last step. It is too high for me to reach. What am I to do?"

You can pray: "Father, please help me to be a better person."

That is a most powerful prayer. "Better" includes everything you want to improve—body, mind and spirit. Your affairs will improve automatically. "Person" includes all that you are. It is confession, repentance, and seeking salvation. It can be a prayer of utter faith reaching the believe-receive intensity that produces results. I can testify to the changing of many lives through this one simple prayer.

So, think it through. Perhaps you'll discover the fact that God *can* depend upon you! If so, you will be able to take all the other steps and completely overcome all fear.

We explained the working of the first five steps in the previous chapters. We named steps six and seven. But we still must look at how they work out in order to complete our master plan for overcoming all fear.

Step six: when a fear arises *face the worst that could happen*.

Step seven: After you face the worst that could happen *be willing for it*—the worst—*to happen or be so,* or continue.

For example:

Let us consider the problem of ill health in old age. This is the way the steps are taken.

1. Look at the problem and name it: sickness, or ill health.

2. Look at the fear: threat to life.

3. Face the worst that could happen: death.

4. Now, be willing for it to be so. This is done by meditation and prayer that lead to higher realization. On this problem we can say:

God is responsible for my life after the transition called death. That is out of my hands. It is God's business and I can be very sure that He has taken care of it before I was born. Father, you gave me life and sent me into the world. I will trust you to take care of me now and take me on into a new life in the next experience you have prepared for me. If it is time for me to die then I die happily, in peace, with songs of praise and thanksgiving.

5. Having faced the worst and been willing for it to be so, you now proceed to ask yourself this question: *Then what?* You are willing to die. Then what? Then where is life itself that was in you? Continue to question and you will be forced back to the beginning: God. Then you will see that it is not death that is the worst enemy

or threat, but the annihilation of the Self, the personality, the You of you. That is the final fear. That is the worst that could happen. Because that is the threat to the greatest of all our urges, or desires—eternal life with our individual Self intact. So we come to the rock bottom of the matter. We face it. We say, "I shall not only die, but shall cease to be, forever." Face it. Accept it. Be willing for it to be so.

6. But continue to ask yourself, Then what? Your soul will begin to give you the answers that will wipe out your last fear. Because finally, all fears are folded in the fear of death and the beyond death. Persist: Then what? Until you get the answer. It will come. Finally you will see and can say, *"I was made to last forever."* You will have reached through to truth.

The chronological steps of overcoming fear—from step one through step nine—will be found in the last chapter, on "How to Get the Most Out of This Book."

9

Land Beyond the Darkness

Neither tears nor fears shall remain . . . the stairs always lead up.

> *I am the light of the world: he that followeth me shall not walk in darkness, but shall have the light of life.* ST. JOHN 8:12

When one of my former students who had done an outstanding job of changing her life heard that I was writing this book on overcoming fear she came to see me. She came, she said, for the express purpose of persuading me to include the little fictional story that had helped her so much.

"Please tell them about the 'Land Beyond the Darkness.' That little story you wrote did more to help me overcome my fears than all the solemn and profound fact teaching you handed out to me. It is easier for me to think in pictures than in rules. When I was trying to break the habit, your story helped me to put the drink down instead of taking it. All I had to do was to think about those people on the bridge. It kept me dry a month. After that I was able to stay sober. But I still use the story. Please put it in your book." I promised. It has helped a good many others. So here it is, with the hope that it will help the reader to overcome any fear he might have left.

LAND BEYOND THE DARKNESS

Once there was a man whose name was J. J. Smith. He was sixty-four years old, had a beautiful wife, two married sons, four grandchildren and two lovely unmarried daughters still at home. He loved them all dearly. He lived in a beautiful house, owned three expensive automobiles, his own airplane, and a great deal of money. Mr. Smith had been a good man, a church member all his life and thought of himself as blameless. He had started in life as a poor boy and was a self-made man. But now he had reached a state of problems that was beyond him.

First, Mr. Smith began to lose money. In a few years he had lost a great part of his fortune in bad investments. Friends had turned against him. He was threatened with fines, imprisonment and disgrace growing out of a business mistake and tax problems. All this had brought on a serious heart ailment and Mr. Smith's doctor told him he had not long to live. His desire was to put all his affairs in order for his loved ones.

On a late summer afternoon Mr. Smith sat alone on the porch of his summer cabin looking out over the great blue lake below and raising his gaze to the gray-blue mountains beyond. But they gave him no help. He had gone up there alone to think things through so he started to look inside for his answers.

"It must be my own fault, somehow," he said aloud. He thought of the problems of his children. "They have picked up my fears," he decided, going over his long list of worries, anxieties and fears. For two days Mr. Smith had been reading his Bible and praying for guidance. "I am somehow wrong," he cried. His faith in God remained. Like Job of old he declared, "Though He slay me, yet will I believe in Him."

Mr. Smith went to bed at dark and fell asleep at once.

About midnight, Smith felt a presence in the room. At first he thought it was a servant or a member of his family. Then he remembered he was in the mountain cabin, alone.

"Who is here?" he called out.

"I am a friend, a Guide," a voice near him replied. "You cannot see me, Mr. Smith, but I came to help you."

"Thank you, sir," said Smith. "I could use some help."

"Come along then," said the Guide.

Smith felt a hand on his arm. He arose and started to walk from the room, the unseen Guide leading him.

Suddenly they were standing on what appeared to Smith to be a wide bridge. In the darkness, Smith could see the cement flooring on which he stood, and a ceiling high above his head, made of narrow wooden boards, painted sky blue. The bridge was about a hundred feet wide. There was a low iron railing on either side. Beyond and below the railings there was water, dark and fearsome to Smith. It stretched away and beyond, farther than his eyes could follow.

"Where are we?" Smith asked, considerably alarmed.

"We are on the Bridge of Life," the Guide replied. "Look ahead. Can you see the end in the distance?"

Smith peered anxiously and shook his head. "No, the horizon closes in with the fog. I can see only about ten feet or so."

"Look back of us," said the Guide.

Smith turned around. Fog shrouded the view beyond a few feet.

"Let us take up our stand here, and watch," the Guide directed.

They moved over to the railing at their right which Smith noticed was made of iron and painted green. As soon as they were settled and still, Smith saw moving forms going past them headed in both directions along the bridge. As his vision cleared he said, "They are people! Men, women, children!" He noticed they all seemed stooped over, some slightly, some bent almost double. Even the young children walked with their heads down on their chest. Some stumbled, some moved slowly, some hurried, but all moved.

"Look closely," said the Guide. "Did you ever see people like these before?"

"No," Smith exclaimed in fear and astonishment. The people were now passing close by him. In all ways they resembled normal human beings except that their faces, hands, their clothing—down to their shoes and up to their hair or hats on their heads—bore splotches of color. Smith quickly saw that there were three colors: red, blue and yellow.

"What do the splotches of color remind you of, Mr. Smith?"

"Camouflage—during the war," Smith replied. His memory was sharp. He had seen service in the armed forces and had never quite recovered from the horrors he had witnessed and participated in. "But not the same colors. Just the idea."

"Yes," said the Guide. "They are camouflaged with their fears. We cannot see the real persons beneath those coverings of fear."

"What is the matter with them?" Smith asked, still amazed and now alarmed.

"They are just normal people," the Guide explained, "but here, in this place and light, the fears that ruin their lives show through. The people on this level are all suffering from three-phase fears. They suffer from threats to life, love and liberty. Look at yourself, Mr. Smith."

Smith glanced at his hands; pushed his arms out in front of him. He was speechless at what he saw. He too, had splotches of red, blue and yellow. Between these ugly splotches—as on the other fellow travelers on the bridge—were the normal flesh and clothing colors of life.

"Now look closely, Mr. Smith, at this man who is approaching us. You will see what he is thinking about," said the Guide.

A large man, so overweight that he was following his stomach, wearing a summer tan suit and a white straw hat with a black hatband, was approaching them. He came quite near. Smith studied his face which was drawn in worry. He was splotched all over with red, blue and yellow. In many places, Smith now noticed, the colors overlapped so that there were green, purple and various shades of the combinations of the three primary colors. He wanted to ask the Guide about this but just then the big man leaned over the low railing, and appeared to be trying to make up his mind whether or not to jump over into the dark and threatening water below. Smith felt such concern for this anguished man that he momentarily forgot his own fears and said, "What troubles you, sir? Can I be of help to you?"

The big man did not answer.

"He cannot hear," said the invisible Guide. "You do not see the real man here, Mr. Smith. You see only *his consciousness*. His ability to hear is back with his human body wherever it is. He is here in consciousness on this level because he has three-phase fears. Now, look again. You will see what he fears—what he is thinking about."

Smith concentrated on the big man in the straw hat, still leaning over the rail. Presently he became aware of forms all around the unhappy man. The forms became sharper in the dark and fog. Smith could now see many objects around the still hesitating man, apparently trying to make up his mind.

"It looks like a house is falling on him," Smith said excitedly, as the forms became sharp and clear in outline.

"Yes, his home is on his mind. He is about to lose it. Note the color of the house, Mr. Smith. It is made up of blue and yellow which shows green. His fears threaten both his status and his liberty. He has money problems. Do you see anything more?"

"Yes—there are some women around him. Beautiful, but they are *threatening* him. And there are papers—they look like legal documents, and oh, my goodness, there is a policeman hovering over him!"

"Yes," said the Guide, "our fat friend here has many problems on his mind and many fears in his heart. But he is not aware that he has brought them all on himself."

Just then a large dark object became clear enough to be seen. It looked like a tall thin man in a dark robe, a man with something in his hand. It was a scythe, such as farmers once used to cut down grain.

"The grim reaper," Smith gasped.

"Yes, our companion here is afraid of death. He will not jump over. Do you see yet another object around him?"

"Now I do! Chains! What large links they have. They are hanging above him, and some hanging from his hands. Some encircle his feet."

"The chains mean that the man has entangled himself by his thoughts, by the wrong methods he used to satisfy his good desires, and by his wrong desires."

By this time Smith could see not only the load of fears each person carried as he passed near him; he could hear the sounds of their fears, thoughts and feelings. At first it came to him as a low hum. It increased into louder mumbling. It went on to shrill noises. It then rose in pitch to cries, and shrieks. Some words of the people were very distinct: "I am afraid . . . " followed by naming their fears. Some were of hatred, resentment, remorse. Others were mouthings of plans for revenge that would stop the fears which tormented them. The voices of the children seemed to reach Smith over the others. He could hear their tears and fears. He began to feel tired and sick. "I can't bear these cries much longer," he said. "Oh, if only I could help them. Especially the children."

"Let us go up higher to the next level," said the Guide. As he spoke he put an invisible hand on Smith's arm and they began to move away from the railing, to walk forward on the bridge.

Presently they came to a great double door that was painted in the three colors Smith saw all around him. Each door was twenty-four feet high and six feet wide. As they approached, the doors parted at the center and silently slid open. Smith felt himself propelled through the open way across a foyer and onto the lowest steps of stairs made of hard gray cement.

"We must climb the stairs to the next level," the Guide explained.

Smith looked up. The stairs stretched up and up before him. He could not see the end of the flight. He felt he just couldn't make it.

"You have to take only one step at a time," the Guide encouraged.

Smith put his right foot upon the step in front of him. He at once felt better. He lifted his left foot. He saw people on the stairs beside and above him. As they climbed higher and higher Smith noticed that some of the colors of the splotches were fading.

"Yes," said the Guide, "we are going up to a higher level of consciousness. We are approaching the level of two-phase fears."

Smith noticed the people nearest the top of the stairs now had only two colors. As they approached an open door which led onto another bridge like the one they had left below, Smith paused to examine his hands and looked down at his feet. He had only two colors now: splotches of red and blue. He asked the Guide what this meant.

"You are entering a level where you have colors of only two fears—those having to do with life and with love," the Guide explained. "You have overcome your fears of threats to your liberty. Different people have different fears. But only two basic fears on this level."

Smith felt lighter in spirit and body as they neared the top step. People were crowding through the open doors before them, and turning to the right. Smith and his Guide followed. Smith noticed there was more light and much less noise here than on the former level.

"This is a big improvement," he said, gratefully.

Here again were crowds of people, going in both directions, all of them splotched with two colors, either red and blue or blue and yellow or red and yellow. Again, there were overlapping splotches of these primary colors so that there were many shades and degrees of shades of fears. Smith watched with great interest and began to recognize persons he had seen on the lower level. A certain man and woman who walked along hand in hand, seemed less stooped and bowed down than they had been on the lower level. Each had two color splotches, but their colors were different. Smith asked why it was.

"They each have only two fears," the Guide explained, "but their fears are different. The man has a life and liberty fear. His wife has a life and love fear. Study these people more closely," the Guide advised. "Listen. Can you hear anything different from what the three-phase-fear people were saying on the lower level?"

Smith concentrated as they walked along. "Yes, I seem to hear a note of hope in their voices."

"You do hear it," the Guide assured him. "Look down the bridge ahead of us. Can you see the end of it?"

Smith squeezed his mind in thinking and squinted hard but he could not see the end of the road. "It ends in a blur of fog," he said.

Just then an odd assortment of people came hurriedly toward them and passed on.

"That looks like a family group," said Smith. "Old men and women, younger men and women and five children. We saw them all before. They seem cheerful on the outside, but they all have those splotches of fear. How is it that they pass us by again?"

"Because they are traveling in a circle. That is why you cannot see the end of the bridge in the distance. It curves just beyond your sight. Come, I will show you. The bridge is only a space of time in circumference. Until people learn how to overcome their fears they may spend all their lives on one level of consciousness, traveling around and around. That is why you see them moving in both directions. Some entertain fears from morning till night while others entertain them from night until morning."

"Oh, how dreary," said Smith. "I will take your word for it. I'd rather go up higher than to travel any farther on this level. Why move in a circle?"

"Good," said the Guide sounding happy. "All right, there is the door ahead of us."

They moved toward the big double door which was like the one on the lower level. It, too, parted in the center and slid silently open as they approached it. Again the stairs rose up and up before them. This time Smith was eager to start climbing. There were fellow travelers beside and above them. The nearer they came toward the top the more Smith noticed the colors of the splotches were fading. "Look," he cried happily, holding out his hands, "only *red* splotches left!"

"Yes," said the Guide, "as you ascend in consciousness you know more and more truth. Truth makes you free. More and more of your chains of fear around your feet—ideas that keep you from walking toward success—will fall away the higher you go."

As they neared the top step Smith received an idea that nearly swept him off his feet. "My friend," he said, speaking so rapidly that he stuttered a little, "would it be possible just to skip this level entirely, and go up to the next one? I mean, do we have to look on the level of the one-fear people? Can't I understand it now, without experiencing it? Still, I will do as you say," he added respectfully.

"If you get your lessons well learned now," said the Guide, "you will have them for the rest of your life. It will not take long to stay a little while on the third level, where you will see people with splotches of only one color. It will be educational."

"Whatever you say," Smith agreed politely, but he sighed a little.

They were then turning to the right on the new, or third level. What the Guide had said proved true. All the people—walking in both directions, some fast, some slowly—were normal-looking beings except for the splotches of color. Some had red splotches, others had blue and still others had yellow splotches. But everyone had only one color.

Smith was so eager to go up to the next level that he began at once to look for the stairs. "Do the stairs always lead up?"

"Yes, indeed," the Guide replied.

"You mean that if a man works out of one level he never descends to it again?" Smith asked, hopefully.

"If he *really* works out of it," the Guide replied. "For a new and higher level of consciousness once attained never is lost. Yes, indeed," he repeated warmly, *"the stairs always lead up."*

Just then they approached the high double doors. "Oh,

I am so glad they will open," said Smith. "We don't have to open them ourselves. We just have to walk up to them."

The doors did open and they walked through and started up the stairs leading to the fourth level.

Smith's first reaction, when the doors at the top of the stairs opened before them, was one of joy. Everything here was light. He could easily see over the railing on either side of the bridge, down to the water below. Now it was sparkling in the sunlight. It appeared friendly, no longer dangerous. Then he saw the people. They were all dressed in white. He could see the faces of only a few of them because they were all going in one direction. But those he did see were happy. The people seemed to be glowing from a light within themselves.

"They are all lighted up," said Smith, wondering.

"Yes. They have the Light that is born in every man. The problem is, to get fears out of the way so that the light can show through and show a man the way to go, and what to do. For the Light gives information as well as reflects on things so that they are seen. Turn now and look back at the oncoming people. Notice that they are all going in one direction, straight ahead."

Smith turned and faced the approaching people. Every face was aglow with an inner light. All were dressed in such radiant white that the garments seemed to have a life of their own. The people were orderly, as if marching to music, and toward some great event that was more important to them than anything they ever had experienced in life before. Some came so near him that he could see the happiness in their eyes—the excitement, yet the serenity in their faces. Each person wore a golden chain about his neck. From the chain hung a heart made of gold which glinted in the light.

"They are happy," said Smith in a whisper of awe. "They are happier than any person I ever have known. Are they the dead?"

"Oh, my, no," said the Guide. "Like all the others, they are just normal people. But these have risen so high in consciousness, have learned so much truth that they are absolutely free from fear. If you could see well enough you would see the ideas they carry with them, like those on the other levels. But their ideas are not of fear. They carry mental and spiritual patterns of the things they want to do, to be, to know and to have. They have learned how to create in thought form first in order to control what will come into their lives in heavier form, or reality, later. You notice the heart of gold which they are wearing? This is a symbol to remind them to keep their heart with all diligence for out of it are the issues of life. Whatever they think about will become manifest in their lives. This is the lesson they have learned. If you could see the ideas around them you would see that they are all good, all made out of love. If you could see clearly you'd see their plans of good for others. Why shouldn't they be happy? They are busy building more stately mansions for their Souls."

"Where are they going?" Smith asked. For, again, he noticed they were all headed in one direction, marching

LAND BEYOND THE DARKNESS 159

eagerly. Too, he saw that the great wide path stretched before them, out and out, and that it was crowded with the white-robed figures, but the path did not curve.

"They are not traveling in a circle," Smith observed. "Where are they going?"

"They are headed for the *Land Beyond the Darkness*," said the Guide. "In that Land they live from a high consciousness, a life completely without fear. Remember that what you see here, John Jacob Smith, is not living people at all. It is the consciousness, or spirit level of people who are still on earth. As people rise in consciousness they tune in or walk on that level. On that level they meet others in the same tune or consciousness height."

"Are they Christ persons in the making?" Smith asked eagerly.

"All people probably are Christ persons in the making, if they so choose," the Guide replied. "The difference is, these people you see here have already reached a high state of consciousness. They do not fear anything on earth or anything yet to come. They know something for sure. What they know is that they were made to last forever, that God loves them, now and ever shall, and finally that liberty—or complete freedom—is their destiny if they so choose. They are walking toward that time and place where they will experience the glorious liberty of the Sons of God. They will dwell in the *Land Beyond the Darkness,* which is the land of everlasting light."

"Do I hear music?" Smith asked.

"Yes. Their combined thoughts are so harmonious they

make music," said the Guide.

"Oh," said Smith, happily, tears choking his voice, "Oh, what must I do, what *can* I do to be like them?"

"You must learn the truth," the Guide replied, "and you will find that you are one of them, John Jacob Smith. Remember to fear no evil. Believe only in good. You will find that you are one of them."

"How did you know my name?" Smith asked, still gazing at the bright and happy throng of journeying people.

"John means brotherly love. Jacob is one who wrestles with ideas. Smith is one who works at his given task. All your names fit you so well that all may read them," said the Guide.

Just then Smith caught sight of yet another door. "Where does it lead to?" he asked anxiously.

"It leads up," the Guide replied. "Up and up forever." His voice seemed to Smith to be trailing off into the distance. "The stairs always lead . . ." The voice of the Guide trailed off into silence.

The light grew brighter and brighter. John Jacob Smith suddenly realized he was lying in his own bed, in his mountain-cabin room. The bright sun was streaming in at his eastern window. Smith arose and walked to the open window, looked out and welcomed the morning. "Thank you, Father," he said aloud. "Thank you for the abundance of good you have given me."

The fears and worries of the day before came flooding back to him. He put a hand to his throat as if to ward them off. His fingers closed on a metal chain. Trembling, he lifted the chain from around his neck and held it out before him. From it hung a heart of gold. Smith stared at it dumfounded. He read the engraving on the heart:

There is nothing to fear.

The chain and the heart glinted with the light of the sun. It began to dissolve and mix with the sun's rays. When the last particle had gone Smith turned from the window, his mind made up.

"I will seek the truth and live it," he said. "I will come free from all my fears and help my family and others to do likewise," he promised himself and God.

Now, John Jacob Smith was a man faithful to a promise. And so, like Job of old, God gave that man more than he had in the beginning.

10

How to Get the Most out of This Book

You have attracted this book to you or you would not have it in your hands. What do you want it to do for you? It came to you in answer to a need of your own, or to help you help someone else in whom you are interested. If, while reading it you felt you'd like to give it to a certain person who came strongly to your mind, follow through. Serve as a channel and give that person a copy of this book. To do so will help to build your own self-confidence and self-respect and set up vibrations of love around you.

We—the world—must learn how to overcome fear or be overcome by it. We must learn how to get fear out of the consciousness of men before it kills all men. For fear is man's greatest enemy. Not bombs and nuclear warfare, but the *fear that drives men to perfect and to produce* fifty-megaton bombs as a defense against fear itself—this is our greatest enemy. The more we help others to overcome fear the less fear we will have to overcome in our own lives. This is important to us. Doctors tell us fear is "more contagious than the measles." And fear is at an

GET THE MOST OUT OF THIS BOOK 163

all-time high around the world because desires for good are at an all-time high.

If you have read this far the book is for you. Why delay success? Let us get to work at once.

1. *Set your stage for action.*

Obtain a hard-cover, three-ring notebook and a good supply of paper to match to be used in *Project, You.*

2. *Obtain your own copy of this book.*

Many people borrow a book from their local library and read it only once. But the serious student, the person who truly desires to change his whole life for the better must *mark and keep* and make truly his own the book he studies. Never loan it out! For as you work with it on your own problems you will be building into your book invisible vibrations which will prove invaluable to you. You do not want the vibrations of others and their problems in your copy. If you think there is nothing to the vibration idea, I respectfully refer you to two case histories in my book, *How to Use the Power of Your Word.* One concerns a house built with evil money and what happened to those who lived there. The other concerns an American girl and her American soldier husband who had to live in a house in Germany formerly occupied by the Nazis. Get a book of your own and keep it for yourself alone.

3. *Read the book several times before you start to work.*

Don't expect to get the most out of this book with two or three readings. You do not change your life in a few hours or days. Allow time for growth. Use a pencil and mark lightly the passages in the book that have especial meaning for you. Each reading will show you new meanings that before escaped you. This is a guide for growth. You will want to erase some markings and make others.

4. *Know where you stand.*

Many people are fearful because they have false ideas about themselves. They compare themselves unfavorably with others without taking all points into consideration. Or they listen to unwarranted criticism and believe it. Paul Deutchler's parents (Chapter 4) convinced him he was sick, or different, and a less person than other boys his age even when he was very young. This was not true but young Paul believed it and it nearly ruined his life. Don't let this happen to you!

Taking an honest, frank inventory will place you where you actually stand and give you a starting point for improvement. Write out a history of your life. Let out all the rope. Underline your successes and failures, your fears and faiths, your good and bad habits, the positive and negative people in your life. You can be sure negative people have fear. Then subtract a negative from a positive until you have a final balance. Work with your facts until you place and really know yourself. Be sure to include your formal education, religious training, background of reading and your likes, dislikes, your search for truth, what makes you happy and what makes you sad. Get an accurate picture of the physical, mental, spiritual you. It will help you to imagine someone is asking you the kind of questions I ask my students. Or pretend you are writing your life story for me. Please do not neglect to make your inventory. You are not ready to start to work for a better future for yourself until you understand your past and present place.

5. *Accept yourself as you now are.*

Bad conscience makes cowards of us all, as witness the story of Mrs. Pollard in Chapter 1. She "lived with a ghost," she said. If there is anything wrong in your life, right it. But no matter what your inventory shows you, accept yourself as you are. Even if you have been to prison? Yes. Even if you have failed all your life? Yes. Don't quarrel with your present situation nor unduly condemn yourself for your past mistakes or failures. Just make up your mind to make good. Now.

If you have a serious conscience problem, or a simple one that bothers you seriously, then go through the ritual (given in Chapter 1, with Mrs. Pollard) of confession, repentance, and making whatever restitution you can and then accept God's forgiveness. Remember, God made you out of Himself. That means you were made out of pure love. But you have worked to the place of free will. If you used it in a wrong way to fulfill a good desire it will bring regret or fear or both. Mrs. Pollard's desire for love of her husband was good. Her way of fulfilling it was a mistake. Look at yourself and your mistake, if you have made one, in that light. Know God already has forgiven you even before you ask. But asking will help *you*. Forgive yourself. Forgive everyone else involved and, in prayer, ask their forgiveness. Then feel free, with a new life to begin.

6. *Now set your new goal.*

What do you want of life from here on? Write it out in your notebook. Start with what you want most, then your second most wanted desire, and on down. Make a "big bold list," as did the Barrows in Chapter 2. Your list will change from time to time. This will show your growth. Your over-all objective will be to raise your consciousness level. This will be taking place as you win point after point of daily needs and desires fulfilled.

7. *List your fears by name.*

You now know your desires. What seems to stand in the way of fulfilling them? Make a list of your current and long-range fears. Trace each fear to its basic desire group. Desire for life leads to need for money. Then the basic fear of not enough money is loss of life. Now you know how and where to work. Giving the fear the color, seeing the splotches of fears will help you to identify them quickly and overcome them.

8. *Discard false modesty.*

You have found yourself, set your goal, and named your obstacles. Now, reexamine your goal. Think about those people in Chapter 7 with a dream in their heart. Is your dream big enough? A big demand brings big supplies and heroic courage. Make a large and worth-while demand upon yourself. We live in that kind of age.

Many talented and capable people are held down by a false belief that they should try to appear smaller than they are. In Chapter 2 we saw this in the life of Jim Barrows, who thought of himself as "grasshopper size." And again, in Chapter 3, Edna Rigger felt her faith was only "penknife size." Many so fear the pain of failure that they never attempt to do the big things of which they are capable. Or they fear criticism of those close to them. You cannot overcome fear until you learn to value yourself, determine what you want of life and then go after it. The great teachers have always told us this. For example:

Emerson says: "Take the place and attitude to which you see your unquestionable right and all men acquiesce. The world . . . leaves every man . . . to set his own rate. Hero or driveler, it meddles not in the matter. It will certainly accept your own measure of your doing and being whether you sneak about and deny your own name or whether you see your work produced to the concave sphere of the heavens, one with the revolution of the stars."

If your life history and your inner desires show you the makings of a hero, don't settle for being a driveler. Be as big as God intended you to be. Trying to reach for the stars of achievement will unfold your dormant faith as you go along.

9. *Build your consciousness with new facts.*

Finding new information, breaking up fear-thought habits, replacing them with fearless ones are the keys to raising the level of your consciousness. Your ultimate goal, remember, is that upper level of White-Light Faith, as seen in the story, "Land Beyond the Darkness" (Chapter 9). You must work at it. A definite change takes place. If you had a bucket of muddy water and continued to pour a stream of clean water into it, the bucket would soon contain only clean water. Just so you can fill your conscious mind with facts by reading, which go down into the subconscious and change fear to working faith. A good way to do this is to memorize affirmations. The rhymed jingles found in all my books (except this one) will help you. Copy those that help you most into your daily-work notebook.

10. *Now you are ready to achieve.*

If you already have the preceding five of my books in this series you are ready to go to work by using the nine steps of overcoming fear which are as follows:

Table of steps in overcoming fear as used in this book:

1. *Analyze your problem* for possible hidden fears. Or acknowledge and name the fear you have.

2. *Analyze the fear* until you have uncovered the false belief that gave rise to it.

3. *Find new information,* facts, truth that will set you free from fear. (The first three steps are found in Chapter 1.)

4. *Live with a purpose,* or set a goal big enough. (See Chapter 3.) This is what Edna Rigger had to do.

5. *Learn quickly to trace, place and erase* your fears before they start to develop fully. Naming them by the three primary colors will help you. (See Chapter 4.)

6. *Face the worst that could happen.* Name it, examine it.

GET THE MOST OUT OF THIS BOOK

7. *Be willing for the worst to be so,* or happen or continue. (These two steps, six and seven, are seen at work in Chapter 5. They are worked out in example in Chapter 8.)

8. *Trust God to take you through.* (See Chapter 7.)

9. *Be one on whom God can count,* by trying earnestly to become a better person. (See Chapter 8.)

Success is a circle. The thought, desire, belief and asking go out from you, collect after their kind and come back to you. After you consciously work with spiritual laws for a while, you will begin to see this process actually taking place. Like Edna Rigger you will be able to say, "I name it. Life brings." Both the good and the bad. The keeping of a record of your trials, successes and failures in your living notebook will help you to watch your growth and this will greatly encourage you. Be sure to have a section in your notebook marked: Answered prayers. Turn back to that list when the going gets rough. It will help to increase your faith instantly.

If this is the first of my books you have ever read:

You may need some background work in order to get the most out of this book and in working with *Project, You*. So with humility and good conscience I present to you a bit of material which I feel certain will help you in your life-changing program.

This is the first of my books without a preface or message to the reader. Knowing something about the author and why I write books should prove helpful to you.

Born and reared in a good Christian home—Methodist—I had a very childlike understanding of the Christian religion, which I lost in college. I did not know it then, but I threw out the baby with the bath water in giving up all religion and church. But later, in 1926, my life was saved through prayer; a little later still, I was saved from being a cripple as the result of the accident which nearly took my life. In gratitude, and wonder, I set out to learn the truth about the power of prayer, to find God, to determine what was the truth of the Christian religion, and what to teach children as a way of life. For one thing, I had been taught that higher education was the answer to all human ills. But in college I learned this was not so and it took me years to recover from the shock of the kind of people I met in college. I did not know such people existed. A good education without the knowledge and daily use of spiritual powers and laws can lead to utter frustration, demoralization, sin, crime, sickness and all manner of evil. Life must have meaning, purpose, or there is no reason to live.

So I set out to learn. Part of the learning—experiences in working with my own problems and the problems of others—became a series of articles published in *Unity Monthly*, a magazine of the Unity School of Christianity. These enlarged, later became my first book, *Change Your Life Through Prayer*, published in 1945 by Dodd, Mead and Company.

Unless you already know a great deal about scientific prayer I respectfully suggest that you get this book. It

GET THE MOST OUT OF THIS BOOK 171

lays down the foundation for the life-changing process. It shows why prayer works sometimes and seems not to work at others. Actually there are twelve parts, or tenets, of the law under which the power of prayer works. For *prayer is a power* and all power is locked in law. Our necessity is to learn to use the power within the laws of its nature. Otherwise, it will not, cannot work for us.

Dr. Alexis Carrel said:

Prayer is the most wonderful form of energy that one can generate . . . the only power in the world that seems to overcome the so-called laws of nature.

Charles P. Steinmetz said:

Some day the scientists of the world will turn their laboratories over to the study of God and prayer and the spiritual forces . . . when this day comes the world will see more achievement in one generation than it has in the past four generations.

Anyone who is trying to change his life and the world through prayer is helping to bring that day closer. Learning about prayer is both a duty and a privilege. The twelve parts of prayer are not all given in that first book. They are put together for the first time in Book V, *How to Live in the Circle of Prayer,* along with the "Circle of Prayer" chart with instructions for use. But Book V should not be studied first by the starting Truth student. They should be taken in the order in which they have been written.

Book II of the series is *Change Your Life Through Love*. This is where Edna Rigger (in Chapter 3) had to work and it is where the whole world will have to work and learn and live—or perish. The law of love is the highest of the spiritual laws as Christ stated and the outcome of our using the powers God has given us, and our free-will choices in life all hinge on whether we have worked within the law of love or against it. With our free will we can bring evil upon ourselves just as easily as we can bring good to ourselves, as many of my case histories in this book will prove. For example, read the story of the woman whose grandson, aged eight, had been placed in a mental institution. Her story showed me generations of hate and evil, broken laws of love. The boy was the "sole heir" to two tremendous fortunes. Sins *are* visited upon the third and fourth generation unless someone knows enough to stop them. Be sure to learn the law of love *before* you start a prayer program.

Book III, *Change Your Life Through Faith and Work*, takes up where Book II left off. The law of creating, or changing or acquiring, is simple enough. It has five parts: desire, asking, believing in faith, and receiving, or accepting the answer when it comes. Many never learn how to accept or receive. Since the answer to all prayer hinges on our ability to *believe we will receive,* this is the place where we must work. Our need is to get everything out of the way that keeps us from believing in

GET THE MOST OUT OF THIS BOOK

utter, childlike faith. Christ taught us to become as "little children" in our relationship and dependence upon God the Father. He also taught about the powers within man and how to set them *safely* into motion. We can never get away from the laws involved. Work has become an unpopular word in our day. Yet to think is to work. We are working all the time whether we know it or not. Our need is to make conscious effort with a predetermined goal. Unless our work is in tune with our prayer we defeat our prayer project and then are likely to think God's answer was "no." Yet all scientific prayer is answered, just as the electric light will go on every time, if we have met the laws concerning it. The law cannot say no. We get instantaneous healings when we have all parts of our prayer in line with the laws under which it operates. We also get *the evil that can destroy* us, if we use scientific prayer for an evil purpose.

If anyone doubts this, let him read the story of Judith in my fifth book, *How to Live in the Circle of Prayer* in the chapter, "Prayer Outside the Law of Love Is Black Magic and Fraught with Danger." There are other case histories in my books which prove the same point. History is filled with such examples from life.

Those first three books were written to prepare the reader or the students (I no longer accept individual students) for the fourth book which probably is the most important of the entire set so far. It is titled *How to Use the Power of Your Word*. I insisted that my students get the necessary groundwork before trying conscious use of the power of their word. We are, of course, using it unconsciously every time we think or speak or when we feel strongly about a matter. We all come to earth filled with this power which we cannot turn off. We can learn how to use it correctly so that it will produce the good we desire and avoid the evil we do not want. To try to use this power without having learned the principles in the first three books would be like the child trying to solve problems in algebra without knowing his multiplication tables. Many people think that because they have always owned a Bible and have read it now and then they understand the spiritual laws. But results in their lives prove they do not understand. I have yet to receive a student who knew about the power of his word when he first came, and this includes seven ministers I have worked with, and many good fellow Methodists.

Do you think preachers do not have problems? In my Book III, on faith and work, you will find a case history of a preacher, pastor of a wealthy and fashionable church who had "lost his religion" long before he ever became a minister and nearly lost his health and mind but was saved by new information, truth (our point three in the nine steps, remember) that set him free from fears, sense of guilt, need for punishment, confusions and doubts.

Book V, *How to Live in the Circle of Prayer*—and make your dreams come true—contains the twelve parts of prayer as previously noted. Now it may well be that the reader knows a great deal more about the spiritual laws than the writer. I can only present what I know to be true, a proven way of life that leads to peace, plenty, happiness, success and Soul growth. While I know that these five books have helped thousands, I still do not want the reader to feel that he must rush out and buy them. I am not telling him to do so. The point is, many who write me, having read one of my books, report that there is no large bookstore nor library near them, and they cannot examine the other books. "What is in it?" they ask. "Should I get it for my studies?" I don't know. It all depends upon how much you already know. The most I can do here is to give enough information to help the reader make up his own mind. People write me their problems and ask, "Do you have a case history that covers my need?" All I can do is to make suggestions.

So: Everyone of my books contains a complete case history of overcoming problems of *physical health* and most of them have several examples with instructions.

The mental-illness cases that have proved helpful include the woman who spent a fortune pretending she was sick and wound up in a mental hospital but eventually "learned her way to freedom." Perhaps the most difficult and most detailed mental case I have yet reported, and one of the most successful in outcome, concerns Edward, told in *How to Live in the Circle of Prayer*. All my books have a chapter or teachings on overcoming mental illness.

Each of my books has a chapter on prosperity or working with the law of increase and abundance. Some of my best examples are in the fourth book, *How to Use the Power of Your Word*. Men seem to prefer it above the other three. It has more examples, references and cases than any other. It also has the best affirmations and more of them, than I have put in any of the others. Many readers find help in the rhymes and jingles, memorize them for constant, daily use. For example:

> *Showers of blessings are falling on me*
> *I claim as my own all the good that I see.*

This jingle enabled one man to see good where before he had not. The law says we may claim for our own as much as we can see—believe in our heart and accept in our consciousness. The man learned to overcome fear and turn seeming defeat into unusual success by sending out the idea that good was coming to him in showers. People began to admire him for his courage, to see worth in him they had not seen before. New opportunities "showered down on him," as he said. He came to believe what he said and so it worked for him. The above is from the book on using the power of your word.

Another jingle from the same book was used by a man who was trying to make his words become profitable servants:

> *I always have plenty to use and to give,*
> *I will always have plenty as long as I live.*

GET THE MOST OUT OF THIS BOOK 177

Saying it is already so is a very high form of asking, saying "let there be," as Mrs. Pollard came to realize (in Chapter 1).

Our objective ever is to fill the consciousness with the fact that good already has been received in *idea form*. Our firm word then becomes flesh, or reality, and dwells among us. The prayer is answered.

For the woman who thinks she is unattractive, or cannot win and hold good and honest love, or the woman who has led an immoral life and wants to change, or the woman who has a daughter who has "gone bad," I recommend the story of Jenny in *Change Your Life Through Love*. Jenny has become a classic. People write to me, asking about her, from all over the world. She was one of the most hopeless cases I ever undertook and one of the most successful in the end. No one knows how much a woman can do when she makes up her mind and works with the power of love.

If your fears have to do with Communism, "creeping" socialism in America, and welfare statism, you will probably find help in *Change Your Life Through Faith and Work*. A whole chapter is devoted to this modern problem and how the individual can handle it. From here on we are faced with the Iron Rule or the Golden Rule way of life. And the whole world is drawn up on one side or the other except those neutrals who have not yet made up their mind which side they will join. This fact was true when I wrote this book and I found it is still true when I made my recent one-woman survey. Both sides are trying to get the neutrals to join them. When this book was first published Roger W. Babson, known to millions for his business successes and inspired living, gave it a full-page recommendation saying he believed it would help to overcome Communism.

In defense of all that "bragging," I want to explain that it was the result of several years of intensive research on my part. I belonged to many freedom clubs, appeared on radio and television on behalf of freedom and mailed out thousands of folders to alert and inform a seemingly sleeping population. Well, they are not asleep today. Learn what to do, start to do it and your fears will vanish.

Finally, the first book of the series, *Change Your Life Through Prayer,* still outsells all the others and is now in its eighteenth printing. Perhaps it gives more help than the others. I don't know. Or perhaps people realize they should start at the beginning if they hope to change their lives and make their dreams come true.

One of the real helps for the earnest student, and especially the younger person starting out in life, are the many quotations in my books of what the great have said and done. Many of these bits of wisdom and records of deeds of greatness are now lost to the modern generation unless they know how and where to research for them and have endless hours to do so. Youth, I find, needs to feel that life has meaning—that they are going some place, for a definite purpose—and some instructions on how to be sure they are headed right. Why hurry, as long as you are on the wrong road? I believe the sickness of our age, so deplored, talked about, and written about, has no basis in itself. We have not trained our youth, have not instilled in them a big enough reason for living, have given them no heroes to follow. It is as simple and as tragic as that.

Well, we must close now. And so, dear readers, dear precious children of God, I leave you now with love. I still work in prayer every day for all my readers wherever they may be, whoever they are, known or unknown to me. Should I go home before you do, I feel certain I can do even better work for you from the other side. Students of life, searchers of truth, you are a glorious company and I am happy to be permitted to be with you.

So look up now. And let your heart be lifted up. There is *nothing bigger than God!*